MW00480346

HEY, I FORGOT TO TELL YOU...

Hey, I forgot to tell you...

WHAT YOUR PARENTS WISH THEY'D TAUGHT YOU ABOUT MONEY

TERRY LINEBERGER
AND KELLY LAUTERJUNG

LIONCREST
PUBLISHING

COPYRIGHT © 2018 KELLY LAUTERJUNG & TERRY LINEBERGER
All rights reserved.

HEY, I FORGOT TO TELL YOU...
What Your Parents Wish They'd Taught You about Money

ISBN   978-1-5445-1175-7 *Paperback*
       978-1-5445-1174-0 *Ebook*

*To our family, friends, and clients. Thank you
for your support, inspiration, and stories.*

To Addison, the next generation.

CONTENTS

FOREWORD

BY RABBI DANIEL LAPIN

There are tennis players receiving assistance from the government's many welfare and entitlement programs, and then there are many tennis players who receive no public assistance. There are those who keep their bodies fit and trim through physical activity on the dole, and there are also many healthy exercise enthusiasts who support themselves without government assistance. Among welfare recipients we can find happy, cheerful people, animal lovers, and grouchy malcontents, just as we find these categories of folks among those who take care of their financial needs independently.

Clearly, playing tennis or liking animals does not keep one from becoming financially dependent upon one's fellow citizens. Almost every type of person can be found among those who live off the public purse, with two exceptions.

The only people almost never seen on government welfare

rolls are those who understand how money works and those raised or living in normative nuclear families. It seems that the portal to prosperity leads through marriage and family along the byways of financial literacy, while the path to poverty bypasses marriage and money awareness.

That is what excited me when I learned that Terry and his daughter Kelly were writing this book you're holding in your hands. Not only are they a beautiful father-daughter team, they have also invested years in understanding how family works, how money works, and how the two work together. If you've ever wondered how much of your financial life to share with your children, the answer is here. If you've asked yourself whether purchasing someone a gift has to fit into your family budget, the answer is here. If you've been uneasy about unresolved inheritance questions, the answers are here.

For years, Terry and Kelly have been using their technical expertise in money and finance to advise their clients, and they have been doing so with great wisdom as they recognize the important role of family in financial affairs. They also recognize the crucial part that finance plays in family matters.

But it's all rather counterintuitive, which makes this book so valuable. People go through high school and enter their twenties having been taught to read, drive, and dress somewhat appropriately, but never having heard a word of instruction on money or marriage. They presume you meet someone, fall in love, and eventually have a baby. There you go: instant family. They assume you find a job, make money, and have no more worries. The problem is that it seldom works out that way.

In fact, building a forty-story building, an airplane, or a ship enjoys a far higher rate of success than building a marriage or a business enterprise. Precisely because money and marriage seem so misleadingly simple, people ignore the available information.

There are plenty of books on money, just as there are plenty of books on marriage and family, but there are not many books about the two together. Reading this book will make you feel you are part of a warm and wise family receiving the guidance and counsel you need from people you intuitively trust. I was so happy to be asked to write this foreword, because my entire career has revolved around making available to people of every background the permanent principles and timeless truths of money and its interactions with the parts of our lives we care about most. Go ahead and start into this book, get to know Terry and Kelly, and benefit by applying their lessons in your life.

You've written a marvelous book, Terry and Kelly, and I thank you for inviting me to be a small part of it.

Warmly,
Rabbi Daniel Lapin

Author of *Thou Shall Prosper: Ten Commandments for Making Money* and *Business Secrets from the Bible: Spiritual Success Strategies for Financial Abundance*

INTRODUCTION

Jack is an intelligent, college-educated thirty-year-old who hasn't settled into a career yet. He's currently unemployed and doesn't have medical benefits, so his parents pay for them. Jack wants to start saving as soon as he gets another job, but he doesn't know how or where to start—he doesn't even know if he *can* start. He has a large amount of credit card debt, so he'll have to spend a good portion of his salary to pay it off. Jack is stuck in a vicious cycle, and his parents are concerned.

This scenario may sound like a case study or a fictitious example. Unfortunately, it is all too true. Jack's parents are our clients. They aren't alone, either. We have many clients in their fifties and sixties with adult children in their twenties and thirties. Like a broken record, they tell us the same things over and over.

"My son has a steady job and makes great money, but he doesn't participate in the company's retirement plan."

"My daughter is working, but she never seems to have any money."

"My kids are in debt, and I don't know if they'll ever get ahead."

"My kids want to buy a house...but can't seem to get money for a down payment."

The most common problems we encounter with young adults are large amounts of credit card and student loan debt, lack of savings, and lack of participation in company-sponsored retirement plans. Some have too many credit cards, and others struggle to keep up with expensive car loan or lease payments.

After seeing these patterns with young adults, we realized we needed to dig deeper and figure out why they are struggling with debt and failing to make ends meet. And if we consistently see these problems with our clients, how many more people are out there wrestling with financial decisions? As we were moved to help families address financial responsibility with their children, we felt the need to write this book. We want families in trouble to get on the road to recovery—and the ones just starting out to avoid trouble altogether.

If you think it's too late for your son or daughter, let us encourage you. It's never too late to begin teaching and demonstrating healthy financial habits and behaviors. And if you're that son or daughter, you can change your financial situation. We're here to help!

TERRY'S STORY

I was born in a poor, rural area of North Carolina. My mother was just fifteen years old, and later went on to have two more children.

My mom was wonderful; she gave us love and encouragement and was a smart, hardworking woman, but she only had an eighth-grade education. She didn't have the skills or means to give us certain kinds of guidance. She did, however, teach me many basic principles of finance. They weren't hard concepts to teach—they were our reality. We didn't buy things we couldn't afford. We didn't have access to credit back then, so we only spent money on what we needed—we had to have the money in the bank or in our pockets.

My mom always encouraged us to save, so when I started working at a young age, I began saving right away. I can honestly say I have never spent an entire paycheck; I have always saved a portion. I probably still have the first dime I ever saved, and I continue this savings habit today.

I joined the Navy when I was seventeen. It was my only option. We didn't have the money for me to go to school. Instead, I spent six years working on nuclear power ships. I was always interested in finance, but my time in the Navy ignited a passion for it—my eyes were opened to options and dreams that previously had seemed unattainable. I met my lovely wife, went to school, and continued my education after the Navy. Although we had two young daughters, my wife supported me through college, graduate school, and in the early stages of my career.

I always enjoyed reading financial publications like *Forbes* and *Fortune* magazines, as well as the *Wall Street Journal*. I read books about Warren Buffett and other great leaders, and I followed Zig Ziglar closely. In fact, since my father had been absent for most of my life, Zig Ziglar became a father figure to me. He taught me what it meant to live a life I could be proud of. Through his lessons, I began to understand the role money played in my life and how it affected long-term goals.

Thankfully, my wife and I agreed on specific life values, and we aligned our goals and priorities to achieve them. When we had differences of opinion, we had open discussions and made compromises. People took notice of my financial decisions and began asking me for advice. Many told me I should become a financial advisor. So, I went on to get an MBA, and I've been advising clients for over twenty-five years. My very first clients are still with me today, and I can't imagine working in any other profession. This job has always been rewarding, and I find even more joy in it now that my daughter Kelly is my business partner.

KELLY'S STORY

My parents are the embodiment of hard work and thoughtful decision-making. They rented houses, saved money, and didn't drive fancy cars. We had a small, eight-inch TV in our family room. I was okay with that. As the firstborn, I was very attuned to the work it took to make money. I understood a large income develops over time, and so does the lifestyle that comes with it. I'm proud to have witnessed my parents' hard work and success.

My parents were open and transparent about our finances, and this was a different experience than what most of my friends had. If Dad had a good month, we went out for dinner to celebrate. If money was getting tight, we stayed home more often and found alternative ways to entertain ourselves. We didn't have lofty expectations, and we had a clear picture of what it looked like to manage finances.

Our family has always been open about all matters, so talking about money was never an issue; it never caused any discomfort. My parents didn't disclose the dollar amount of their monthly bills, but they were always transparent about where our family stood financially. Dad acted as my financial advisor, and I kept my savings and investment accounts with him. There was no getting around conversations about money because I had to discuss every withdrawal with him first. We didn't have these discussions because Dad was trying to control my money—he was lovingly teaching and guiding me in my financial decisions. He was my accountability partner for my savings and investment goals.

My upbringing still influences the way I make decisions. I grew up having conversations about money with my parents, and I still do today. For major financial decisions, my husband and I often work together with them to figure out what's best. We evaluate our income, how much we have in savings, and what we want to accomplish.

I'm aware of the unwise financial decisions my peers make, and it's heartbreaking to sit back and watch some of their choices unfold. Soon after I partnered with my dad, parents came to me with desperate pleas to talk to their adult children.

We recognize an urgent need for this book to open the door to conversations between parents and their adult children. There are many pressing financial topics that need to be addressed for adults in their twenties and thirties. As this generation begins having kids, the issues will only grow in complexity. In writing this book with my dad, I hope to share his valuable knowledge and experience with others and to help young adults get on the road to financial success.

FINANCE IS A LIFE SKILL THAT CAN BE LEARNED

Children won't learn money management skills if it's left to chance. We have to walk them through a learning process. We can't rely on them getting information from outside sources. It's our responsibility to teach them.

As adults, we are in contact with money every day of our lives. From a young age, kids are also in contact with money on a regular basis, whether we realize it or not. Managing money is a life skill, just like reading or driving. If we don't teach our children how to read, we can't be angry or surprised when they don't succeed in school. Similarly, we wouldn't hand them our car keys without teaching them how to drive first.

They receive an allowance, carry lunch money, participate in fundraisers at school, and run lemonade stands in the summer. There are many teachable moments in daily life—it's not difficult to orchestrate a lesson about money; we simply need to recognize the opportunities.

Usually, if parents fail to teach their children certain life skills, they will learn them elsewhere, at least to a degree. Unfortunately, financial responsibility, budgeting, saving, and home buying aren't taught in school. We must intentionally guide our children in these areas.

We've never met a parent who said, "I want my kids to

have credit card debt. I don't want them to save any money. They don't need to know how to balance an account." Parents care, and we must take the necessary steps to teach our children how to manage their finances.

As teens, we start itching for independence. When I first started making decisions on my own, I wasn't allowed to just do all the fun adult stuff like driving, moving to college, or staying up late. All the other "#adulting" responsibilities came with it. My mom showed me how to cook and do my own laundry, Dad taught me how to pump gas, etc. Personal money management went hand in hand with my newfound freedom, and my parents set me up to succeed with my finances. They taught and led me through the processes of budgeting, saving, giving, and personal banking.

HOW TO USE THIS BOOK

There are several ways to use this book. It can be a conversation starter between the two generations of parent and child. It can also be used as a how-to guide or an idea generator. This book is for families and individuals, as well as for parents of children of all ages, young or old. It's for young adults starting their journey to financial independence, and for the parents who want to see them through to success. This book is for anyone who wants to start making better financial decisions.

If you're thirty years old and out on your own, you should

learn and implement the concepts we discuss in this book. If you are the parent of an adult child, you should introduce these ideas to them. It's best to start teaching children money management when they're young, but it's never too late—start now.

In each chapter, we'll present one of seven healthy aspects of finance that you must implement for financial success. We'll dig into ways you can establish the habits of saving and budgeting. We'll walk you through typical budgets from different phases of life and show you the progression and changes of each one. We'll discuss the importance of participating in retirement plans and how much you should contribute. We'll help you understand appropriate levels of debt and how to use credit responsibly.

It's critical for your family as a whole to grasp these concepts, not just your child. We want to help you create a support system for one another.

GETTING STARTED

If you were our client, or we had just met with you for the first time, we would ask you to share your financial values. We need to know what is most important to you—the factors that influence you when making decisions about money. What are the basic and most vital reasons that drive your financial choices? What are your main concerns? Safety? Prosperity? Do you fear losing money? Are you living beyond your means?

We'd also ask you to establish your goals—what do you and your family hope to accomplish? Do you want to make sure your kids' college is paid for? Do you want to retire at a certain age? Do you want to be independent as an older adult, so your kids won't have to support you?

Identifying values and goals is the best way to begin the process of financial management or debt recovery. These two steps are key in determining how you will budget, save, and spend. They serve as the starting point for every individual, couple, and family.

You can use the Discovery Diagram to answer these two important questions. We've provided sample answers from clients to help guide you. Additional questions are included in the diagram to help you begin creating a plan as well.

DISCOVERY DIAGRAM

Security: I don't want to worry about running out of money.
Independence: I don't want to be a burden to my kids.
Freedom: I want to do the things I want, when I want.

It's important to me that our two kids go to college. I'd like to fund four years of in-state tuition.
I've always dreamed of owning a boat. It will cost $15,000.
We want to take a family vacation every year. We expect to spend about $5,000.
We bought a fixer-upper, so we have home projects that we plan to do over the next 10 years, costing $50,000.

1. What's important to you about money?

2. Why are those things important to you?

3. What are you most worried about when it comes to your money?

4. What would you like to change about yourself and how you approach money?

5. Where do you see yourself in 5 years? 10 years?

6. What would you like to acheive with your money?

7. If you didn't have to work anymore what would you do?

8. What do you envision for your life? For your family?

12. How often do you review your financial plan?

13. Why do you save and invest the way you do? How did you decide which investments to choose?

14. Who do you turn to for advice? What made you choose that person?

9. What are your sources of income? How is that likely to change?

10. How do you currently save? What do you need to do differently?

11. What benefits do you receive from your workplace?

I started saving at work to take advantage of the company match of 3%. A co-worker recommended using the target date fund.
I'm not very knowledgeable about investing so I just check my balance every so often. As long as it's going up I'm happy.

I work full-time. I make $50,000 per year (salary). Once I'm done with my MBA, I expect to be making $75,000.
I save 5% via payroll deduction into my 401K plan and I save $200 a month into a savings account.
I have great medical coverage through work. An HSA account, and a life insurance policy two times annual salary.

The answers to these questions vary greatly among clients—there is no typical answer. The important thing is to identify what is important to you and your family. Then, commit to a plan, and begin taking steps to change your financial situation.

BUDGETING

ALIGN SPENDING WITH VALUES AND GOALS

"Through discipline comes freedom."

ARISTOTLE

Once you've used the Discovery Diagram and answered the questions to help establish your values and goals, the next step is to create a budget. What comes to mind when you hear the word *budget*? Do you feel intimidated? Confused? Do you picture yourself spending hours crunching numbers? Do you think of penny pinching and putting restrictions on your money? We ask our clients if they budget, and the answer is usually no, followed by a "the dog ate my homework" type of excuse.

"It's too overwhelming."

"I don't have time, and I'm too tired to do it."

"After I pay my bills, I don't have any money left to budget."

"My spouse will blow through a budget anyway, so why should I bother?"

In reality, budgeting should not be intimidating, confusing, or time-consuming. It's not meant to be restricting, either—in fact, it gives you freedom. Budgeting is deciding in advance where you will spend your hard-earned money. You earned it, so you decide what to do with it. Budgeting allows you to prioritize your money, so you can save and spend it in ways that are meaningful to you, and it helps you achieve your most important values and goals.

IT'S NOT A SPENDING PROBLEM

Clients often tell us they don't know where their money is going every month. They're either living paycheck-to-paycheck or spending their entire paycheck before it even hits their bank account. They are unable to save, and they are frustrated. They feel stuck.

Most people think they have a spending problem when, in fact, they have a discipline problem. They'll end up spending the same amount of money no matter what; it's just a matter of how they will spend it. We need to be disciplined enough to spend our money on what we *really* want.

A big part of the problem is that people aren't keeping track of how and where they spend. How can your money be in alignment with your values and goals if you aren't aware of how you are spending it? People end up spending money on what is enticing at the moment, and not on the things they've prioritized as most important.

For example, a client says they have a goal of retiring at sixty-five, paying off their mortgage in five years, and taking their family on a Hawaiian vacation. However, they aren't on track to accomplish any of those things, because they spend all their money on designer clothing, and they eat out often.

Budgeting is a tool that creates discipline and puts you in the driver's seat to reaching your goals. It puts you in control of your money. You can't let spending happen passively; plans and decisions should be made in advance. It's your money, you've worked for it, and you have the privilege of deciding how to spend it.

Having a budget implies you're living within your means. We don't suggest budgeting for more than you make. The purpose of budgeting is to determine where you *have* to spend your money and where you *can* spend your money. Budgeting allows you to spend money on what you really care about; it aligns your spending habits with the values and goals you've identified.

VALUE: COLLEGE EDUCATION
GOAL: GRADUATE DEBT-FREE
STATUS: ACCOMPLISHED

My wife and I have been living on less than what we make for a long time. We began saving at a young age, and it gave us the freedom to tell our daughters they could go to any college they wanted to. Our savings gave them the ability to graduate from their schools debt-free. We were able to support our family in this way because we had the discipline to save. It wasn't always easy—we had to say no to many purchases because we knew they would interfere with our goals. But discipline will ultimately give you freedom. An undisciplined person is stuck in a financial prison. They're unable to accomplish their goals, and they never know if they will have enough money to cover their expenses.

VALUE: BE DEBT-FREE
GOAL: LIVE WITHIN OUR MEANS
STATUS: ON TRACK!

My husband and I have been married for four years. We budget routinely every two weeks, right at payday. It's safe to say we have more freedom than many of our peers, yet we don't feel robbed of any experiences or luxuries. Yes, we can be frugal, and we save a lot of our money, but it's because we've identified goals that are important to us. Staying on track has allowed us to travel, purchase new cars with cash, and buy new furniture for our home without going into debt. Budgeting is not as restrictive as people think it is—it creates freedom.

NEWS, SOCIAL MEDIA, AND FOMO

Technology and social media provide conflicting information that can create unrealistic financial expectations. There's a certain "keeping up with the Joneses" mentality prevalent today.

When my dad was young, he watched a highlight reel of the world's events on the nightly news. Today, news is accessible twenty-four hours a day, seven days a week. We now have convenient, immediate access to information, but that can hurt us when we are unable to decipher the truth in the constant stream of data. Media, bloggers, and Facebook friends have commentary to offer on every topic imaginable, and there are an infinite number of sides and opinions to every story. It's easy to get confused.

We're inundated with false reports in the news and media, and for some reason, we choose to believe everything we read. So, what should we believe, and how do we determine what's true? One day, we read we should contribute 10 percent of each paycheck to our 401(k); the next day, we hear a Roth IRA is the best option. We need to take the time to dig into the information and do proper research—especially when it comes to making financial decisions.

Social media can also have a negative influence on how we compare ourselves to others. We see perfect pictures on Facebook and Instagram or read tweets on Twitter, and we develop a bad case of FOMO (fear of missing out). FOMO tends to hit us hard, since technology and social media are so prevalent in our lives.

We feel pressured to have or do certain things because of what we see online.

FOMO can be perpetuated by the illusion that our peers are more successful or have a lot of money. However, I have yet to see a social media post that says, "My parents gave me money for a down payment," or "Grandma paid for my new car." It's unlikely they will announce that in an Instagram hashtag. As outsiders, we have no idea whether or not a peer is truly successful, or if their grandmother is supporting their lifestyle. It's easy to compare a friend's highlight reel to your worst days.

It's important for us not to be swayed by what friends and peers are doing, no matter how amazing it may seem. If friends are buying new houses and cars, good for them, but it might not be the best option for you right now. Buying a home is a life-changing decision, and there are many factors to consider. Do you have a down payment saved? Are you ready for the responsibility of owning a home? Do you know where you'd like to settle long-term? FOMO can't be our motivation for major life decisions that will have huge financial impacts.

Determine your own goals and priorities, and remind yourself of those when you start to wrestle with FOMO or discontentment. I've often had feelings of embarrassment when I thought I was falling behind. But my husband and my parents have helped me to stay focused on my own goals—not the goals of my peers.

TRACK YOUR SPENDING

Once clients identify their financial values and goals, we ask them to track their spending for a month and return to us with the results. Tracking helps them become aware of how much money they spend and where they spend it. We ask them to track everything down to the last penny, including bottled water purchased at gas stations and change spent at vending machines. It may seem tedious, but it's only for one month.

Then, we review the results to determine if their current budget and spending align with their values and goals. Were they surprised by the amount of money they spent or how they spent it? The answer is often yes—they are surprised. Their spending didn't align with or help them achieve their goals, values, or priorities. They didn't realize they had spent so much on subscriptions, cable, and Netflix. They wished they'd put more into their child's college fund or donated more money to charity.

Tracking your spending for the first time can be an eye-opening experience, and it provides an ongoing visual cue. If you track your spending for a month and find it doesn't align with your goals, you can see where and how much you've been spending on nonpriorities. How can you reallocate your spending? How can you save for what's most important to you and your family? Budgeting in this way can help you with your next step: making changes.

The more people there are in a household, the greater the complexity of the budget. There are simply more people who can derail it. Mom could spend too much on groceries; Dad could spend too much on golf. Extracurricular activities for the kids could cost a fortune as well. It's rare for people to think about the future consequences of their current spending, which makes budgeting even more important for families. They need to make sure their budget aligns with both short-term and long-term goals. For example, will all the years of paying for soccer turn into your kids racking up student loan debt later?

If you are unable to save for long-term family goals because of current expenses, then you may need to revisit your budget and see where adjustments can be made. It is important to remember that spending doesn't always have to change. Sometimes our family goals, needs, or expectations for the future need to be adjusted. Long-term goals are not set in stone; just like our lives, they are always evolving. It's important to have a balance between current family values and long-term goals, and your budget should reflect that.

NO MORE AFTERTHOUGHTS

It's important to budget for routine monthly costs, but it's equally important for you to budget for expenses that don't occur on a regular basis. We budget for rent, utilities, and car payments, but we should also consider expenses that appear less frequently. A few examples are:

- Gifts
- Car registration and maintenance
- Property taxes
- Home repairs and maintenance
- Insurance premiums
- Tuition payments
- Vacation and entertainment

Gifts and the periodic expenses listed above are typically left out of budgets. These items are afterthoughts. Christmas falls on the twenty-fifth of December every year, but when it arrives, everyone acts surprised. Nobody seems to have money set aside to buy Christmas gifts. They end up busting their budget, using credit cards, or scrambling to gather money. As a result, December can be an overwhelming, stressful month for many people. It doesn't have to be that way.

GIFT BUDGETING TIPS

My husband and I decide in advance how much we want to spend on gifts for the entire year. This includes Christmas, birthdays, and other occasions. Then, we set a bit of money aside each month for gifts in our short-term savings. This is separate from our checking account and long-term savings.

My wife and I do things similarly. At the beginning of the year, we list all the people we want to purchase gifts for, and we decide how much we're going to spend on each person. If we say we're spending twenty dollars per person, that's what we do—we don't spend forty dollars. If you happen to be buying gifts for sixty people in a given year, that can add up to a significant amount of money.

SPECIFIC GOALS

I have friends who are saving for their child's college fund. They put $100 in on the day the child was born, and the grandparents contributed some money over the course of the year. The child recently turned one, and the account has close to $500 in it. That's a great start.

However, I did a financial review with the parents recently, and they were overly excited. They thought that after market growth, the $500 would miraculously turn into enough money to fund the first year of college. They are incredibly disillusioned.

Of course, there will be market gain (we'll talk about that in Chapter Three), but you must have a specific goal in mind. Investing random amounts and hoping for enough gains to pay for college is not a sound strategy.

When setting goals, you should start by identifying a specific amount or cost, and then devise a plan to achieve it. But how do we determine how much to save for each expense?

First, look at the goal and work backwards. Start with the full future cost and then figure out how much you need to save each year to accumulate that amount. Then, break it down into a smaller monthly sum. In this way, you can save reasonable amounts and the goal doesn't become overwhelming.

For example, our family wants to purchase a new car in five years that will cost approximately $30,000. In order to set aside that amount and meet our five-year goal, we need to save $6,000 per year, or $500 per month. We would adjust our budget accordingly, and factor in the $500 a month for future car replacement.

If you don't start with the end in mind, you will most likely fall short. If you throw random amounts at a goal, you'll miss your target. Determining how much you need is simple. If you are saving money for a car, you can find out the anticipated price you'll pay when you intend to buy it. If you are saving for college, look for information about school tuition and fees, including how much the costs are expected to increase each year. Financial advisors can help you create a savings plan once you've specified the goal.

FAMILY MATTERS

It's important for all family members to be on the same page when it comes to the budget. Although each person may have different goals, every goal should be addressed in the budget. If there is disagreement, a conversation should be had to more clearly define the family goals.

Some days, we feel more like marriage counselors than financial advisors. Family members have different expectations when it comes to money, and it isn't always a smooth transition when they begin the budgeting process. We get involved in these conversations with our clients, and we encourage them to prioritize together and come to an agreement. It's important to revisit core family values when discussing family and individual goals—work together to make sure values and goals stay aligned.

When everyone is in agreement on the family's priorities, the budget can reflect the wants and needs of the family as a whole. When everyone is on board with the goals, everyone works harder to achieve them. Family members will uphold the agreement, which means arguments can be avoided on the back end.

It's important for the entire family to understand the budget. If they don't, you run the risk of someone blowing through money, or spending in an area that wasn't agreed upon because they didn't support a particular goal.

I like to encourage couples to make this conversation fun and lighthearted. Go on a date and dream about the future together. Give each person time to share what they want to accomplish or do as a family and let that be the basis for the budget. Start with the vision, and then figure out the numbers.

STRUCTURED FLEXIBILITY

A budget isn't set in stone. Goals and priorities can shift, and there are many situations in life that require a budget to be revisited.

My wife and I have been married for over thirty years, and we've always been in agreement on financial matters. Sure, we may disagree about how much to spend at a particular restaurant, but we've always been united when it comes to our core values and goals. Early in our marriage, we sacrificed vacations, new cars, and cable TV so that we could maintain our values and meet our goals. For us, the priority was having my wife stay home to raise the girls.

Today, we have a fairly predictable, well-structured budget, but there is room for us to be flexible. For example, a few years ago, our church needed some event tables. We offered to purchase some tables and budgeted appropriately for what we thought the cost of the tables would be.

When the pastor and I went to buy them, we discovered the tables cost twice what we had budgeted for. Instead of giving up on the purchase, I called my wife, and we discussed the unexpected price. We agreed as a couple to use the money in our restaurant budget for the month to cover the additional cost. Our priority was to help the church, so we chose to purchase the tables and not go out to dinner for the rest of the month. We achieved our goal and stayed within our budget.

This example demonstrates the power and freedom in budgeting. It provides options. Understanding how much money you make and deciding in advance how you're going to spend it takes the stress out of managing your finances.

It also demonstrates that you can avoid financial conflicts in your marriage through open communication. You and your spouse may not agree on everything, but your core values will provide common ground in your budget.

THE TRANSITIONAL BUDGET

Kelly got her first job as a lifeguard and started making money at the age of fourteen. I asked her how she planned to spend her money and how much she intended to save. She didn't have any expenses at that time, so her choices were simple. She created a budget and figured out how much she wanted to spend on items like clothing, entertainment, and saving for a car and college. This was not just a decision-making process; it was also a teaching process.

High School Student

	Month:			
	Starting Balance in Account:	**$100.00**	**Bill due**	**Responsible**
Savings	Savings – Long Term Goals (College/Car)			Student
	Gifts			Student
Fixed Expenses	Tithe & Giving		1st	Student
	Insurance – Auto			Mom & Dad
	Cell Phone		15th	Mom & Dad
Variable Expenses	Gas			Student
	Eating Out			Student
	Entertainment/Fun Money			Student
	Clothes			Student
	Salon/Beauty Appointments			Mom & Dad
	School Supplies			Mom & Dad
	Total Spent			
	Amount Leftover	**$100.00**		

Fast-forward to college four years later, and my goal was to create a comprehensive transitional budget for her. My wife and I covered the cost for Kelly to attend college, but we didn't write a single check to the institution; we only wrote checks to Kelly. She was responsible for paying her tuition and for living expenses—she had to work directly with school administration and housing management.

We had certain guidelines in place, and she entered her expenses into a spreadsheet. We reviewed the budget together to make sure everything was reasonable and correct, and then I wrote her a check on the fifteenth of each month.

We had a column of items that she would pay for and a column of items that I would cover. As time passed and Kelly began to work part-time in college, the number of items in Kelly's columns increased, and the number in mine decreased. She was expected to pay for all the columns when she graduated and began working, but I wanted to give her time to transition. The reality of adulthood could either catch Kelly by surprise, or she could gradually grow accustomed to paying her own way. I felt this transitional budget was the best way to usher her into her own household.

There's a lot more to college than just getting a degree. It's a time for young adults to learn responsibility and get a real-life preview of adulthood. A transitional college budget is one way you can teach your kids how to manage money, and it's fail-safe. If they screw up, what's the worst that could happen? They won't get evicted, freeze to death, or go hungry. There's no risk involved in using this teaching method. If your child struggles at first, they are still under your wing. It's better for them to learn how to budget while they have your help—and before they are on their own.

Kelly made mistakes here and there, but we had time to fix things; it was never a big deal. She knew if she spent more than we had agreed upon or more than she made at her part-time job, she would have to deal with the consequences, not me. However, it was never a problem. She did a good job managing her money.

It wasn't a problem for me to stay within my budget, because I was told I wasn't allowed to have a credit card—all I had available to spend was the money in my account. I was forced to live within my means.

Month:			
Starting Balance in Account:	**$100.00**	**Bill due**	**Responsible**
Tithe & Giving			Student
Savings – Long Term Goals			Student
Gifts			Student
Car Repairs/Maintenance/Registration			Mom & Dad
Vacation			Student
Tuition & Books			Mom & Dad
Rent		1st	Mom & Dad
Utilities – Electricity			Student
Utilities – Gas			Student
Insurance – Auto/Renters			Mom & Dad
Cell Phone		15th	Mom & Dad
Cable/Internet/Streaming Services			Student
Groceries/Toiletries/Home Goods			Student
Gas			Student
Eating Out			Student
Entertainment/Fun Money			Student
Clothes			Student
Salon/Beauty Appointments			Mom & Dad
School Supplies			Mom & Dad
Subscriptions/Memberships			Mom & Dad
Travel – To and From School			Mom & Dad
Total Spent			
Amount Leftover	**$100.00**		

Row groupings (left margin): Savings (Tithe & Giving through Vacation); Fixed Expenses (Tuition & Books through Cable/Internet/Streaming Services); Variable Expenses (Groceries/Toiletries/Home Goods through Travel – To and From School).

I'm thankful to Dad for helping me establish this habit when I was young, even though it was frustrating for me as a college student. For a while, it even created some anxiety about future bills. I remember moments when I was angry and crying over the phone. I called my mom behind his back and asked her to just send me the money, because I was done with the stupid budget, but she didn't do it.

I clearly remember a time when I had to submit my budget to Dad and tuition was due in two days. I had piles of homework to do, and I didn't get to the budget. I asked him to please send me the money, but he refused. He said the only thing he required of me was a budget, and it was my responsibility to do it. If I couldn't fulfill the requirement, then I would have to deal with the late fees. I was furious! Dad knew I was frustrated, but he didn't back down. He wanted me to learn.

Budgeting during college taught me how the world operates. It gave me a foundation for understanding how to be successful in life. It also motivated me to do well and make money. You have to work hard to excel in your career—nothing is handed to you. I learned that bills are due and need to be paid on time. Your landlord and the utility company don't care if you have an essay due—they need to get paid.

I appreciate that my dad didn't just fork over the money when I asked him to. He did pay my way through college, but I had to do some work for it. In essence, my "job" at that time was to be financially responsible and produce a budget—that was the work that was requested of me in order to get paid. Through that experience, I learned valuable life skills and experienced the reality of cost-of-living expenses.

When we first began budgeting, I talked through it with my dad and asked questions on a regular basis, but it's second nature to me now. It's a habit. I have come to enjoy it, and helping others learn how to budget was one of my motivations for joining his business.

GETTING STARTED

When my husband and I budget, a huge priority is making sure we have money for tithes and charitable giving. Then, we allocate money for all our expenses.

Next, we budget our savings. We have short-term savings for gifts, car repairs, vehicle registrations, and other purchases that may be on the horizon. For example, my husband is a musician—we save so that he can buy new equipment. We're also starting a family, so we have a fund for baby furniture and other related expenses.

Then, we identify long-term expenses. We want to buy a home and establish an emergency fund. We know we'll need a new car one day, so we set money aside for it each month. We paid cash for our first two cars, and we plan to pay cash again when it's time to buy a new one. By planning in advance, we can avoid going into debt for a new car.

All of this might sound overwhelming, but budgeting is very simple once you hit your stride. In fact, keeping it simple is the key to success. I budget twice each month on payday. It takes me ten to fifteen minutes each time. With today's technology, you don't have to budget by hand or use an Excel spreadsheet. You don't even have to do the math! There are various online apps and tools you can download to help you.

The first few months will be a bit time-consuming because you have to select and narrow down financial categories and decide how much to save and spend for each one. We suggest limiting budgeting and financial conversations to thirty minutes or less. It may be necessary to have multiple conversations to pull your budget together. This time limit is especially helpful if you (or your spouse) do not have a lot of interest in the family finances.

We also suggest you don't budget in the following situations:

- When your stomach is empty
- While rushing to make a purchase (especially at the store)
- While arguing with your spouse
- By going tit for tat or trying to "even out" spending between family members

When you first start to budget, you'll need to shift things around a bit. Stick with it, and soon, you will hit what we call the "budgeting zone." It will become automatic. For guidance, refer to the sample budget for a young working professional and a young family.

Young Professional

Month:		
Starting Balance in Account:	**$100.00**	**Bill due**
Tithe & Giving		
Savings – Long Term Goals		
Emergency Fund		
Home Downpayment		
Retirement		
New Car		
Gifts		
Car Repairs/Maintenance/Registration		
Vacation		
Rent		
Utilities – Electricity		1st
Utilities – Gas		
Insurance – Auto/Renters		
Insurance – Disability		
Cell Phone		15th
Cable/Internet/Streaming Services		
Groceries/Toiletries/Home Goods		
Gas		
Eating Out		
Entertainment/Fun Money		
Clothes		
Salon/Beauty Appointments		
School Supplies		
Subscriptions/Memberships		
Hobbies		
Total Spent		
Amount Leftover	**$100.00**	

Savings (Savings rows: Tithe & Giving through Vacation)
Fixed Expenses (Rent through Cable/Internet/Streaming Services)
Variable Expenses (Groceries/Toiletries/Home Goods through Hobbies)

Young Family

		$100.00	Bill due
Month:			
	Starting Balance in Account:	$100.00	**Bill due**
Savings	Tithe & Giving		
	Savings – Long Term Goals		
	Emergency Fund		
	Home Downpayment		
	Retirement		
	New Car		
	Private School or College Savings		
	Gifts		
	Car Repairs/Maintenance/Registration		
	Vacation		
Fixed Expenses	Rent		
	Utilities – Electricity		1st
	Utilities – Gas		
	Insurance – Auto/Renters		
	Insurance – Life		
	Insurance – Disability		
	Cell Phone		15th
	Cable/Internet/Streaming Services		
	Childcare		
Variable Expenses	Groceries/Toiletries/Home Goods		
	Gas		
	Eating Out		
	Entertainment/Fun Money		
	Clothes		
	Salon/Beauty Appointments		
	School Supplies		
	Subscriptions/Memberships		
	Kids Acitivites		
	Hobbies		
	Total Spent		
	Amount Leftover	$100.00	

After reviewing the samples, take the following steps:

1. If you haven't done so already, align your budget and spending with your values and goals. Take time to envision the future and write down your goals and pri-

orities. It's helpful to track your spending for a month to see if your spending aligns with your values and goals.

2. Make changes in your habits and lifestyle to spend more of your money on items of importance. Reduce spending on peripheral, excess, or luxury items.

3. Budget for future expenses, like a new car. Break up larger, long-term goals into smaller monthly amounts.

4. Budget for "nonroutine" expenses, such as gifts and car registrations.

5. Revisit your budget during times of transition, like getting married, having a baby, an adult child moving out, retirement, etc.

6. Finally, be kind to yourself. Remember that budgeting is a process. Stick with it!

The old cliché is true when it comes to budgeting: failing to plan is planning to fail. We believe budgeting is the key to financial harmony. Budgeting alone doesn't mean you will be successful, but it allows you to establish the direction you would like to take.

Determine where you want to go, and create a reasonable plan to get there. Financial advisors can help you draw the map, but we can't drive you to your destination. You may not make enough money to reach all your goals, but at least you'll have a road map for the journey—one that relies heavily, of course, on understanding the value of saving.

CHAPTER

2

SAVING

PLAN TO SUCCEED

"Wealth gained hastily will dwindle, but whoever gathers little by little will increase it."

PROVERBS 13:11, ENGLISH STANDARD VERSION (ESV)

Now that you have a budget in place, you're prepared to begin a plan for saving. Budgeting is the perfect transition into saving once you've established your short- and long-term goals. The habit of regular saving is the most important foundation for financial freedom. It gives you the ability to take guilt-free vacations, retire when you choose, handle life's emergencies, and pursue your dreams and goals. Saving can end the cycle of debt and begin the cycle of financial prosperity.

THE HABIT OF SAVING

While I was in college, I worked part-time. Even though I didn't earn much, I saved a portion of my paycheck every time I got paid. At that time, people could buy US savings bonds out of their paycheck before cashing the net amount, so I also bought a bond as part of my savings routine. Later, I was able to use those bonds to purchase my first home and help fund my girls' college educations. I no longer buy bonds each payday, but I continue to have a systematic savings plan.

Every animal saves. Squirrels store up nuts for winter, bears store up fat, and colonies of ants save food for a rainy day. Even our ancestors saved—it was essential for their survival. When we begin to think of saving in this way—as a means for survival—we understand the importance of setting aside funds for the future. There will come a time when your savings will "save the day," which is why we literally need to save a portion of every dollar we earn. Kelly and I recommend always saving at least 10 percent of your earnings.

The power of saving is often overlooked. Besides building wealth over time, saving gives you options—it's your choice whether or not you spend your savings. Most of our wealthy clients did not become so as a result of winning the lottery or receiving a large inheritance; they grew their wealth by saving diligently. If you take away only one concept from this book, take this one: the difference between the people who build wealth over time and the people who don't is the savings habit.

CYCLE OF DEBT

Debt is a crushing blow to families and has been on the rise for the last fifty years. Some families spiral into debt and have a hard time breaking free. A lack of saving contributes to this cycle of debt. It stands to reason that if we're in debt, our needs exceed normal income, and there's no additional padding. Extra expenses push us deeper in the hole.

The normal month-to-month paycheck covers routine living expenses, but it doesn't cover anything above and beyond, such as buying a new car, going on vacation, or buying Christmas gifts. If you don't have money set aside for these things, and there's no wiggle room when your paycheck arrives, then additional spending can require you to go into debt.

LIFE'S EMERGENCIES

Some expenses are easy to predict. For example, you can identify goals like saving for a new car, a kid's college fund, or a new wardrobe. However, we believe the highest priority goal should be the emergency fund—saving for unforeseen expenses that can pop up and catch us off guard. We recommend setting aside three to six months of living expenses for this fund. (These are your routine expenses such as rent, utilities, gas, and groceries.)

Emergencies are inevitable—something unexpected will happen. We aren't trying to be pessimistic, but we do want to be prepared. We all have emergencies—flat tires, car accidents, medical emergencies, or last-minute travel arrangements. With an emergency fund in place, a personal or family crisis does not have to become a financial crisis as well.

A recent study by the St. Louis Federal Reserve stated the personal savings rate in 2015 was 5.7 percent. This study also revealed that seven in ten Americans have less than $1,000 in savings.* That means 70 percent of people will struggle to come up with funds to replace the tires on their vehicle, something that will happen inevitably at some point. Too many of us are living on the edge with no buffer against hard times.

For example, consider Hurricane Harvey, which hit Houston, Texas, in 2017. Many families were already struggling with little money and savings, and then their homes became flooded. They had to spend money on hotel rooms, replacement vehicles, and new clothes, among other things. The burden was crushing. The best possible way to remain financially secure in times of disaster is to have an emergency fund. Insurance is another tool to protect us in times of emergency that we will discuss later in the book.

* fred.stlouisfed.org

SHORT-TERM SAVINGS

Once you establish an emergency fund, the next step is developing a savings plan for upcoming purchases over the next three to five years.

> ### SAVING VS. INVESTING
>
> Saving and investing may seem like the same concept, but they are different financial strategies.
>
> Saving is taking money and setting it aside to make sure we don't get caught shorthanded.
>
> Investing is putting money into something we expect to grow, so we can live a better life in the future.

We discuss investing in detail in Chapter Three, and we don't want you to confuse saving with investing. We compare short-term saving to "storing up for winter," and since winter comes every year, the key to success with this method is repetition.

EXAMPLES: THREE- TO FIVE-YEAR SAVINGS GOALS

- New car
- Down payment on a home
- Vacation
- New appliances
- Home furnishings
- Hobbies or interests (For example, Dad saved to buy a new bike for triathlon training.)
- Baby (A young family thinking of adding a new member needs to anticipate added expenses.)

PLANNING FOR REPLACEMENTS

We know tires have a finite lifespan, so replacing them after a certain number of miles shouldn't come as a surprise. The same goes for appliances—specific savings used to replace these items will remove a major burden from your life.

You have about ten major appliances in your home—a washer, dryer, refrigerator, etc., and each has about a ten-year lifespan. I used to replace the oldest appliance first in expectation of the dreaded day it would quit, but unfortunately, many of today's appliances no longer last ten years, so I had to adopt a new strategy. For example, I bought a dishwasher two years ago, and it has already broken down. The repair would cost $400, so I decided to replace it instead. It's not the dishwasher's "turn" to be replaced, but by planning to replace one appliance per year, you won't be caught off guard, and you can be more selective about your appliances.

Earlier this year, my wife and I were able to replace our refrigerator in a nonemergency situation. It was over ten years old and still worked well, but we decided it was time to buy a new one. Since there was no time crunch, we shopped around and found the perfect refrigerator on sale for 50 percent off. Had we waited for the appliance to break, we may not have been so lucky.

Big box stores make it easy to buy items on credit, offering them interest-free for five years, but doing so is a risky practice. Saving in advance gives you more options and prevents you from digging into the hole of debt.

THE POWER OF STARTING YOUNG

As children age, parents have less influence on the creation of habits, which is why it's ideal to begin teaching them while they're young. And this doesn't just apply to financial habits. It applies to any habit.

For example, parents help young children establish an after-school homework routine. Maybe they have to finish homework before free time or before they can watch television. Parents don't wait until children are in tenth grade to start this routine; they begin the first day their child has homework.

Parents should work to establish a similar routine with money. Before we can spend it on what we want, we must first put a portion in savings. We teach children to eat their dinner before their dessert, right? We should teach the same with money—first things first. We save before we spend.

If you have teens, you might consider a savings-matching program when they begin saving for a car. For every dollar they save, you'll also contribute a dollar. We've heard this is a very effective strategy, and it can also be used to help your teen save even more. With matching, you reinforce the savings habit and assist the child with reaching their goal more quickly.

What if your child is twenty-five or thirty years old, and they don't have a savings habit? Don't be discouraged. It's never too late to begin. Share success stories and demonstrate the value of automatic savings plans like 401(k) s and systematic savings. You can still choose to offer incentives or rewards for a time, which can help your adult child establish the habit of saving. Remember, the end goal is establishing the habit, not putting a specific dollar amount in the bank.

THE ENVELOPE SYSTEM

Before the girls were old enough to have bank accounts, we used an envelope system to save. They placed babysitting money and other money they earned into one of three envelopes: saving, spending, and giving. They split their money equally among the envelopes.

We did this when the girls were young, but the same principle can be applied if your kids are older. It doesn't matter if they are ten or thirty-five years old; you can always encourage the habit of saving.

TEACHING THE NEXT GENERATION

We recently met with a grandfather and his grandson. The young man was just getting started with a savings plan. He talked about his personal financial successes to encourage his grandson, and also shared the mistakes he had made. Sharing cautionary tales and advice on how to avoid negative situations was powerful and memorable for his young grandson.

This grandfather discusses finances with his grandson frequently, teaching him what we advise. Create a budget, save a portion of every dollar you earn, participate in retirement accounts, etc.

Bringing children to such visits and appointments can be quite meaningful. The grandfather introduced his grandson to us, his financial advisors, and he explained, "These are the people I meet with to help me with my money. These are the questions I ask them." He also introduced his grandson to his CPA. It's a huge benefit for young adults to meet people and learn which resources are available to help them become successful.

MY FIRST BANK ACCOUNT

When I was about ten years old, my parents took my sister and me to the bank to open our first savings accounts. They taught us how to fill out the savings deposit form and talk to the cashier. Later, when I became a lifeguard at age fourteen, we went back to the bank so that I could open a personal checking account.

As soon as I had both a checking and savings account, my dad kicked the budgeting and saving lessons into high gear. We created a system in which a portion of every paycheck was transferred into my savings account, and I would budget the remainder for things like clothes, gas, or entertainment.

I became comfortable going into the bank, talking with the teller, using the ATM, and navigating online banking tools. I also learned to maintain my own financial records by updating my check register for deposits and withdrawals. At a young age, I understood the most important principle of finance: saving. If I received birthday money or Christmas money, or if I earned babysitting money, I put some in savings. In fact, for a time, the family rule (or maybe it just *felt* like a rule) was to always put half of our pay into savings.

Both my sister and I practiced this through high school. Since we didn't need our income for living expenses, it was the perfect teaching tool. And at that high rate of saving 50 percent of our income, we saw how quickly the money added up. It established a strong habit in us, and we assumed all adults saved in this way. We didn't know much about finance at that young age, but we were programmed to save, and we continue to reap the benefits.

Even today, you might say I'm addicted to saving—my husband and I aggressively save toward our goals. Between retirement and a down payment on a home, vacations, and miscellaneous expenses, we save a considerable portion of our income.

GET STARTED NOW (GSN)

You might be reading this and thinking, "That's impressive, but it sounds difficult. I don't think I could ever do that." I once felt that way, too.

When I started saving for Kelly to go to college, I read that tuition cost an exorbitant amount of money. The sum might as well have been $7 billion, because it felt impossible. I thought, "I'll never have that kind of money, so how about I just get started?" I saved a small amount of money and let it accumulate. At the beginning, I couldn't save enough to fully fund the goal, but I could save something, so I got started.

Starting is the key. We call it GSN, or "get started now." If your final goal is to save 10, 20, or 30 percent of your income, it doesn't mean you have to start there. I've completed several marathons, but I didn't go out and run twenty-six miles on my first day of training. Saving is like athletic training—you start by running around the block twice until you work up to a mile. Then, you work up to two and keep going.

It's the same with saving. Start with what's comfortable, and then save a bit more so that it's slightly uncomfortable. When that slight discomfort becomes comfortable due to an increase in income or lifestyle adjustment, bump up the amount again, and keep saving until you reach your goal. For example, start with ten dollars per week. If you can stick with that, within a year it will be easy to save twenty or thirty dollars per week— or more. Saving becomes simple once the habit is established. As Aristotle once said, "Well begun is half done."

IT REALLY WORKS

One of my clients is a friend from elementary school. He is a schoolteacher, and he and his wife were getting ready to have a daughter. They decided she would be a stay-at-home mom, and I recommended they begin saving for his daughter's college. My friend wasn't sure he could do it on his teacher's salary, but he committed to putting money aside each month into a savings account. He put in extra money whenever possible, and he did this for twenty years.

His daughter is now in college, and he recently called to thank me for encouraging him to save money for her education. He still puts money into her account today, even though she's already in school. He's established a lifelong habit of saving and likely won't ever stop. As an added benefit, his daughter has recognized the value of this habit and is a saver as well.

SAVING FOR LONG-TERM GOALS

Retirement is a common long-term goal that individuals plan for. The amount a person should save for retirement is dependent upon the age they begin. The later you start, the more you'll need to set aside. For example, a twenty-year-old just beginning to save should aim to set aside 10 percent of their annual income. However, if someone starts saving at age forty, they'll need to save 20 percent or more each year, since they don't have as many years for the funds to accumulate. They need to make up for lost time.

A great way to grow retirement savings is through a 401(k) or another salary-deferral plan. And, if you automatically increase the contribution by a small percentage each year (like 1 percent), you won't even notice it! We will discuss investing for long-term savings in the next chapter, but we want to mention the importance of getting in the habit, starting early, and automating when possible. These principles are important with any long-term savings goal, not just retirement.

AN IRA SURPRISE

When my husband first started working full-time, we opened up an IRA account and contributed a small amount each month. We added a little extra when he got a bonus. We've also been able to increase his contributions over the years as he's received raises. We recently reviewed his account, and he was surprised by how much had accumulated in a short period of time. We definitely aren't ready to retire yet, but we have a great start.

WAYS TO SAVE

People often struggle to save, especially if they didn't develop the habit at a young age. The easiest way to ensure consistency in saving is to automate your transactions. Using payroll deductions or designating an amount to be directly routed into a savings account are strategies that can lead to success. Limiting access to your savings can keep you on track and prevent the temptation to withdraw funds on a whim. We recommend not having debit cards or checks for accounts with money designated as savings.

Before I joined forces with my dad, my husband and I had our savings accounts with him. Since he was a financial advisor, we asked him to be our gatekeeper. Whenever we wanted to make a big purchase, we had to call Dad and ask him to transfer the money into our checking account. He would ask us what we were doing, if the timing was right, and whether or not we really needed to make the purchase. We appreciated the conversation and the accountability; we had to think twice before transferring funds.

ESTABLISH ACCOUNTABILITY

Accountability was another factor that helped us establish the habit of saving. As kids, my sister and I had bank accounts, and we also had accountability with my dad. He checked in with us frequently and asked about our savings plan, how much we were saving each month, and what we planned to do going forward.

Even when I got my first job after college, my dad asked about my 401(k) paperwork. "Did you sign up for the 401(k)? Did you set the percentage? What are your investment options?" He always had an interest in our finances, and he still holds us accountable to this day.

The principle of accountability is useful in finance, but it's important to pick the right partner. Keep tendencies in mind when choosing your financial accountability partner. Recruit someone who isn't a big spender. This person can be a spouse, a friend, or a family member. It should be someone you can be honest with and someone you respect who manages their own finances well.

An associate shares accountability practices with her brother, and others may partner with friends or parents. Having someone help you filter spending decisions and adhere to self-identified spending limits will protect your hard-earned funds.

Consider following a twenty-four to forty-eight-hour rule. If you plan to spend more than a specified amount ($500, for example), make waiting part of the decision-making process. Call your accountability partner and talk to them about your plans, and then wait twenty-four to forty-eight hours. If it's an impulse purchase, the desire should fade within that time frame. If it's a legitimate purchase, it will still seem rational after the waiting period, and you can proceed with the purchase.

LEARN TO DIFFERENTIATE

When considering financial choices, it's important to differentiate between *needs* and *wants*. *Needs* are purchases that will bring comfort or joy for the long run and should align with goals. *Wants* make life easier or more enjoyable for the moment but may not align with goals. To be successful, it is essential to discern what is important to you in the long run versus what is important to you now. Taking the easy road now tends to make life harder. Conversely, if you put the work in now, life can get easier.

Early in our marriage, my husband and I knew we wanted to save money to buy a house, and we didn't want the house to be empty.

We needed a couch, a bed, other furniture, and appliances. We set a budget to put us on track to buy a house and equip it with the basics. I made a chart of our needs and wants and put it on the refrigerator. Our savings goals were front and center, which was great, until dinnertime when we both wanted to go out to eat.

We had no choice but to consciously look at the chart and revisit our priorities. If we went out to eat, we'd delay the purchase of a couch. The money was either gone (traded for a meal, activity, or frivolous item) or added to our savings account. For example, on nights when we chose not to eat at a restaurant, we transferred the amount we would have spent directly into the furniture fund. Instantly, we were thirty dollars closer to buying a couch.

The visual on the fridge helped us to immediately filter our *needs* versus our *wants*. We had to think twice about choosing convenience in the moment over our family goals. The responsibility was ours, and the goal was always in sight. Writing down your goals and putting them on display is a good method to stay focused on your priorities. There were plenty of nights we didn't want to cook. There were times we wanted to see a movie, attend a summer concert, or take a mini-vacation, but we didn't. Being able to see the reason for our restraint—our listed goals—helped us quickly build a robust home-furnishings fund.

SAVING IS NOT...

We know saving is putting money aside or into a savings

account. Bargains and sales try to pass as "saving," but they won't bring you closer to your goals.

We've all heard someone say, "Hey, I spent $200, but there was a sale, so I saved $100!" That's really just another way of saying, "I didn't spend $300." The person didn't save anything, and they don't have an additional $100 in their bank account. They have $200 less in their checking account. Or, if we spend enough at a store, we earn $100 in store bonus cash. That's a great in-store perk, but it doesn't put $100 into our savings account.

Be careful with shopper loyalty plans. Money can be earned, saved, or spent, and shopper rewards fall into the category of "spent." Remember, true saving is putting money away or sacrificing spending—your savings account should reflect a new, higher balance. It's not saving if the account has less money in it.

BENEFITS OF SAVING

Saving becomes easier as you go along and experience pleasant surprises, like the first time your account reaches $10,000, or you accomplish a goal. Each of those milestones will encourage you to keep going. You will have those surprises. You'll wake up one morning and think, "Oh, my gosh. I'm rich!" You'll look at your accounts—your savings, your 401(k), your investments—add them all up, and be floored by the total. It's exciting and comforting to see funds accumulate. The practice of saving pays off.

FINANCIAL FREEDOM

Saving can change lives and create countless options. It takes the stress away when surprises and emergencies arise. If my wife's car breaks down, we don't have to worry about the cost to fix it; we have the money. We have a sense of security, and we have opportunities to give toward the needs of others. For us, giving is about choices and discernment, not about the money.

When it was time to pay bills each month, Kelly told me she hated having to ask me for money. I said, "Please don't hate asking me. This is one of the biggest joys of my life. I've saved money from the time you were born just to send you to college, and I want to spend the money on your education."

Saving allowed me freedom from worry and freedom to pay for my two daughters' educations. I imagine I could have spent it on other things, but their education was important to me. On the other hand, if I'd needed to use it to bail them out of jail, I would have been less pleased—but still free to use the money as I wished.

A NEW RELATIONSHIP WITH MONEY

Saving creates a change of perspective about finances. When you save for a specific purpose, you don't mind spending money for that reason or cause. You worked hard to earn and save, and it's enjoyable to spend money on its intended purpose.

For example, my husband and I saved all last year for a vacation. We didn't have a destination in mind; we decided at the last minute to go to Mexico. We had saved enough to pay for two airfare tickets and a stay at an all-inclusive resort. We were excited we had the funds in our budget, and it was rewarding to go on a debt-free vacation. It was incredibly relaxing.

Saving makes many of life's experiences much sweeter. It's a joy to give that gift, go on the vacation, or make a down payment on your home because it's not overshadowed by the stress of debt.

STRESS IS NOT AN OPTION

Money is like education in the sense that the more you acquire, the more options you create for yourself beyond just money in the bank. You will have tough times and struggles, but that doesn't need to tear a family apart. Many marriages struggle with finances, and it ends up destroying the relationship—it doesn't have to happen to you or your family. Saving will help you do away with that stress. Now, let's get started.

SAVING: THE MOST IMPORTANT
TOOL FOR FINANCIAL HEALTH

The habit of saving is the key to being successful—start today, and never stop. We can't emphasize this enough. Without a doubt, establishing this habit is the number one thing you must do to become independently wealthy. I have saved a portion of every paycheck since the very first time I got paid and continue to do so to this day. My daughter does the same. Every wealthy client of ours, without exception, has a foundational savings plan, and this is not by chance. Saving is the science of cultivating wealth.

There are two primary reasons to save: emergencies and planned expenses. To get started, first, set aside three to six months of regular living expenses to create an emergency fund. Next, begin saving toward specific goals—be sure to think about both short- and long-term ones.

Once you've identified your goals and devised a plan to save, you're ready to boost your success! It's time to experience the power of investing.

CHAPTER

3

INVESTING

PARTICIPATE IN THE FUTURE

"How many millionaires do you know who have become
wealthy by investing in savings accounts? I rest my case."
ROBERT G. ALLEN, AUTHOR OF THE ONE MINUTE MILLIONAIRE

Some people think of investing as gambling. They picture themselves going to Las Vegas and putting money on red or black, or they think they are taking risks with no predictability of success. Fear discourages people from investing; they're afraid of losing their money. They believe the risk is too great for the potential reward.

The news and media need to keep their material interesting, and what they report can frighten the everyday investor. Their reports are exaggerated, inaccurate portrayals of investing for the average person. We've all heard crushing stories of the speculative investor who purchased investments based on rumors and ended up losing everything. However, that's not how we recommend investing. It shouldn't be a gamble.

We don't want people throwing money at crazy ideas and hoping for a big payday. Our philosophy of investing chooses proven companies that provide products and services for billions of people—innovative companies that create better solutions for all our lives.

THE OPPORTUNITY

People often worry about the market going up or down, how the current presidency will affect it, and a number of other factors. I was born in 1963, and I don't know exactly what the Dow was back then, but let's say it was around 600. As we write this book, it's over 22,000—that's a thirty-six-fold increase. The market doesn't determine our wealth; our choice to participate and our actions do.

Historical Closing Numbers: Dow Jones Industrial Average

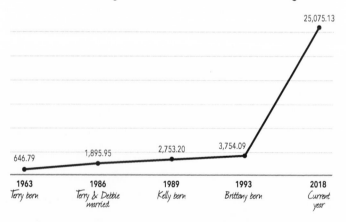

Take a moment to consider the options you have for your money:

- *Leave it under your mattress.* Put one hundred dollars under there, and come back in ten years. You'll still have the one hundred dollars, but it won't be worth as much ten years later, due to the increasing cost of goods (aka inflation). A dollar today won't get you as far in the years ahead.
- *Put it in a savings account.* It will earn interest over time, but probably not enough to keep up with inflation.
- *Invest it.* Put your money in a diversified portfolio of good, solid companies that are growing and earning dividends.

WHAT ABOUT RISK?

Starting to invest can be confusing. Whom should you trust, and what investments should you choose? What about big losses? There are many factors to consider when you begin.

There are many conflicting methods and philosophies of investing, so the first step is talking to people who are doing it successfully—this may be a professional financial advisor, or a knowledgeable individual investor. Yes, it's easy to lose money if you don't invest correctly, but don't let that scare you away. Find a trusted source who can help guide your decisions or offer recommendations.

Secondly, if you automate the process of investing, it will take emotion out of the equation. Emotion is the chief hindrance to logical investing, so if the process is automatic, you will invest regularly. There are options that allow you to invest monthly or at the interval of your choosing, such as payroll deductions and dollar-cost averaging.

DOLLAR-COST AVERAGING

Dollar-cost averaging can take the emotion out of the investment decision-making process. This strategy allows you to invest the same amount of money each period. However, the number of shares you purchase varies depending on the current price of the investment. You'll buy more shares when the price is low, and fewer when the price is high. Overall, the average price per share can be lower than trying to time the market.

As with any investment strategy, dollar-cost averaging cannot guarantee an investor will profit, nor does it ensure against the potential loss of principal. Additionally, dollar-cost averaging involves continuous investment in securities regardless of fluctuating price levels of such securities. Investors should consider their financial ability to continue making purchases through periods of low price levels.

DOLLAR COST AVERAGING

DATE OF INVESTMENT	PRICE PER SHARE	TOTAL INVESTMENT COST	NUMBER OF SHARES
Month 1	$10	$100	10
Month 2	$7	$100	14
Month 3	$5	$100	20
Month 4	$8	$100	13
Month 5	$15	$100	7
Month 6	$12	$100	8
Average Price Per Share	$8.36		

Finally, keep in mind that investing essentially makes you part owner of a company. Choose a company that provides products or services that make your life better, serve the world reliably, and will continue to fulfill needs in the foreseeable future. You also need to know about the management of the companies you choose—are they managed well or shrouded in controversy? If the companies are reliable and well-managed, then most likely, you have made a wise choice.

TEMPORARY VS. PERMANENT LOSS

People worry about volatility—the ups and downs of the market. "It's up twenty...now it's down twenty." These are only temporary gains and losses of capital; only panic can turn these distressing moments into permanent losses. And that is what we want to avoid in our investing: permanent loss of capital.

An example of a permanent loss is purchasing a home that is overpriced and then selling it at a loss. We want to avoid permanent losses of capital, but in order to do that, we can't be fearful of temporary losses. In fact, when the market is down, Kelly thinks of it as the ultimate Black Friday special.

This can be difficult, psychologically. We don't feel safe buying when the market is down. We'd much rather buy when the market is going up. It feels counterintuitive, but when it goes down, that's when we should buy. That's why our investment plan must be automated and not based on fear. "Buy low, sell high" is something easily said, but difficult to put into practice.

There are certain stocks I buy every time they fall; I have thresholds. When these stocks go below my threshold, I buy and add them to my position over time. If they never go below the threshold again, it's fine, because I have plenty in my portfolio. If they go up again, great—I make money. If they go down again, I don't panic—I buy it again. I do this, because I am confident these companies will be around for a long time, and they will continue to make money.

Temporary losses of capital are not meaningless. We use them as reminders to check our assumptions and review our game plan. Just don't panic.

INVESTMENT GOALS

We invest to meet our long-term goals—the ones exceeding the three- to five-year time frame of our savings plan. Examples of investment goals include:

- Retirement
- College
- Second homes
- Rental homes
- Vacation properties
- Weddings
- Charitable giving
- Boats or cars
- Big trips
- Major home repairs or remodeling

SELECTING YOUR INVESTMENTS

A common misconception is that stockbrokers are prowling around, always working to sniff out the best new stock. They need to find out what's hot right now. What's fresh and new with explosive growth? We won't discuss all the different products and investments available to you in this book. There are many to choose from depending on your goals, risk tolerance, and assets available to invest. The purpose of this chapter is to encourage you to do the research, talk with a trusted advisor, and step out of your comfort zone.

We believe our morning routines are a good place to start when evaluating investment options. If we take a hard look at the companies we interact with on a daily basis—the ones embedded in our lives—we'll discover they may be the ones we want to invest in.

TERRY'S MORNING ROUTINE

My Sony alarm clock wakes me up in the morning. I get up and brush my teeth with Colgate toothpaste on my Procter & Gamble toothbrush. I do my final rinse with Listerine mouthwash.

I put on my Nike shorts, Duluth Trading Company shirt, Hanes socks, and Asics tennis shoes, and then head out for a run or walk.

I use my Garmin watch to track my distance and pace. I put my earbuds in and listen to my favorite morning podcast.

I return home and make a cup of Starbucks coffee using my Keurig coffee maker. I add Nestlé creamer and have a bowl of Kellogg's cereal.

While I eat my breakfast, I ask Alexa to tell me the morning news on the Amazon Echo, and I check my emails on my Apple iPad.

Before I forget, I take my blood pressure medication made by Pfizer.

Now, it's time to get ready for work, so I use Dial soap in the shower, shave with a Schick razor, dry off with a Costco towel, and apply Procter & Gamble deodorant. Then, I style my hair using Bristol-Myers Squibb hair gel.

I dress in a Nordstrom shirt and a Men's Wearhouse suit. Then, I lace up my Johnston & Murphy shoes and head out the door.

I get into my Nissan car, drive to work on Michelin tires, and stop for gas at Exxon.

Once I get to work, I turn on my Dell computer and use Microsoft applications to check my calendar. Then, I start my workday.

MY MORNING ROUTINE—DECONSTRUCTED

Based on my regular morning routine, I interact with twenty-nine companies before 8:00 a.m., and I'm sure my day is not much different from yours. You may not go for a run in the morning, eat cereal, or drink coffee, but you do have a routine, and it probably has you interacting with twenty to thirty companies—ones that will be around for a long time. Those are the companies you want to co-own and participate in.

By putting your money into these companies, you are not only investing—you are thanking them. Your dollars say, "I want you to stick around. I believe in your products and services. I trust you will continue to work for me as I help build your company."

The morning routine takes some of the fear out of investing, so it feels like a pursuit, not a gamble. I challenge you, the reader, to examine your morning routine and identify the products, services, and companies embedded in your day.

CONSIDER WORLD EVENTS AND PROGRESS

Consider 2017's Hurricane Harvey in Texas. I heard that about 500,000 vehicles were destroyed. How does this relate to investing? We can surmise that people in Texas purchase many trucks and large vehicles.

Car manufacturers will need to make and sell more vehicles

to help people get back on the road, back to work, and back to taking their kids to school.

Society won't return to the days of steam-driven locomotives, gravel roads, and horse-drawn carriages. The cars of tomorrow will be fuel efficient, lightweight, and perhaps even solar-powered. Likewise, the airplanes of tomorrow will go farther on one gallon of fuel than they do today. They'll hold more people, and they'll move faster.

You want to participate in the small or large companies that produce the mechanisms that move the world forward. Government does not create this progress; these advances in our society are created by businesses. So, that's the essence of investing to me: participating in the future.

LIFE-SAVING TECHNOLOGY

When I became pregnant with our first child, my husband and I anxiously awaited the twenty-week ultrasound where we would see the baby's growth and development. We couldn't believe how clear the imaging was! We saw all ten toes, a beating heart, and the cutest little nose.

After our appointment, the doctor reviewed the measurements and information gathered in the ultrasound. Since the imaging was so clear, they were able to detect a few potentially life-threatening complications. At first, I was terrified, but then I thought, "Thank goodness for advancements in technology." Without the clarity of the picture in the ultrasound, these issues could have taken my life in normal labor. Now, we could come up with a plan for alternative delivery options.

This is the very reason why I invest. I reap the financial benefits of companies that do well via dividends and growth, but I also benefit from the advancements these products and services create in our world. It's a win-win situation!

CAN I INVEST ON MY OWN?

When I think of investing in my long-term or bigger savings goals, I think of the relationship I have with my dentist. I brush my teeth every day, but I visit my dentist on a regular basis for checkups. He makes sure I'm on track with my dental care, using the right toothpaste, and flossing. In the same way, we can use our own best practices with investing, but a professional helps bring insight to the big picture.

SHARING SUCCESS

An example of a valuable financial lesson my dad taught my sister and me is what it meant to share in the success of a company. When we were young, my parents and grandparents purchased stock for us in the stores and restaurants we liked, such as McDonald's, Abercrombie & Fitch, and Limited Too. We received the stock certificates as Christmas gifts, and we both had mini-portfolios by the time we turned eighteen.

Dad taught us how to research companies and how they operate. He explained that buying stock supports companies and their products, and that we also participated in the success of those companies.

My sister profited from these lessons the year she chose her own stock. Dad asked her what type of stock she wanted, and she put her thinking cap on. Since everyone joined a gym and began dieting at the first of the year, she wanted stock in SlimFast shakes. She went to the grocery store and found out Unilever was the manufacturer, so she bought stock in the company. Even as a young girl, she could be a savvy businesswoman.

WHAT'S ON THE LINE?

Managing a whole portfolio is a big commitment. Routinely, we see people who have been successful for years when the consequences were relatively small. But after they've funded their 401(k)s for a long time and realize at age fifty-eight they have accumulated a large sum of money, they don't want to mess that up. They don't want to make high-dollar decisions without a second opinion, because the stakes are too high.

If they make the wrong move now, they could be saying goodbye to the retirement income they've been building all their life. So, they call someone to sit down and run through appropriate portfolio options for their stage of life and their goals. Yes, they could continue to manage it themselves, but they feel reassured when they call in the pros for a second opinion.

Portfolio management also takes discipline. Ask yourself, "Am I disciplined enough to take this on? Do I tend to make emotional decisions or respond out of fear?" If you're at risk for pulling your money out of a down market and turning a temporary loss into a permanent one, then seek the counsel of an advisor.

FULL-TIME FOCUS

When I first started in this industry, I studied for eight hours every day. I had to learn many laws, regulations, rules, and requirements surrounding the topics of investing in stocks, bonds, mutual funds, various products, tax consequences, and planning considerations. Investing is a complex field, and it's personal. Unless you're willing to take the time to learn and follow the ever-changing details, you should seek help from a qualified advisor. I'm now settled in the field, but I continue to conduct research for two hours each day.

DIVERSIFICATION

We construct diversified portfolios of stocks, bonds, and mutual funds because we don't want to put all our eggs in one basket. A portfolio should contain a mix of large, medium, and small companies. It should also contain domestic and international investments. We suggest allocating a portion to fixed income (bonds and bond funds) to manage risk, and equities (stock) to achieve growth. Diversification is an art and a science—you create the right combination based on what you want to achieve. No two portfolios will be the same, because no two investors have the same goals or risk tolerance.

I like to compare building a portfolio to following a recipe. First, you decide what you want to eat. Then, you list all the ingredients that go into making the recipe. Notice you rarely add equal parts of anything; you use a cup of this and a dash of that. Once it's ready to be served, you make it exactly how you like it—some people add hot sauce because they like it spicy, while others may prefer things a little sweeter. Or, if you were like me as a kid, everything was smothered in ketchup.

INVESTMENT SELECTION CRITERIA

Be aware of the reason you're investing in a company. Some people simply hear about a stock and go for it, but there's more to consider than just ups and downs. Solid companies are involved in our morning routines, but not all of them are great investments all the time. These companies make great products, but one or two may be improperly managed or overvalued (overpriced for what you get).

For example, let's say you can typically buy your favorite pair of Nike shoes for $120, but you wouldn't buy the same pair for $240. If they were priced at eighty dollars, you might stock up and buy two or three pairs. The investment industry does this type of research to decipher the metrics of a product's reasonable value. There are certain prices that don't make sense for shoes. When $120 running shoes cost $240, it's best to wait.

Industry metrics tell us when a price is too high. Criteria include the price the public is willing to pay and the prices of competitors' brands. Metrics also tell us when to liquidate. When we see our Nikes selling for $240 on eBay, and we have three extra pairs we bought for eighty dollars each, we're going to sell. And we'll make a nice profit in the process. A professional advisor understands those metrics and can help you capitalize on investment opportunities.

WHEN TO SEEK ADVICE

Personally, I think you should always seek advice. If you don't know something, ask. That was a big mantra for us when Kelly joined the team. If you don't know, ask. You'll find out quickly who the best, most reliable people are for giving advice. Asking is much easier than attempting to synthesize a thousand-page book to understand a concept.

Advisors can also help you stay on track and establish team accountability. They have an objective perspective, so they can shed new light on ideas and filter out emotion. They have knowledge and understanding of investing and can manage the portfolio as it becomes more complex.

It can be stressful as portfolios grow, but there is comfort in knowing advisors manage money for a living. We spend our time counseling and encouraging people. We are cheerleaders who also remind clients of their personal goals; we advise and help clients stay the course. The alternatives to investing—sticking money under the mattress or using a basic savings account—will likely leave you short of reaching your goals, and that can be a scarier thought than investing. Remember:

- Don't be afraid! Investing is participating in the growth and development of the companies and products we love most.
- Do your research. Understand what companies stand for and how they are managed.

Hopefully, this chapter has provided clarity and peace of mind about investing. If you still aren't comfortable, call a professional or someone you trust to advise you on how and where to get started, and what you need to be aware of.

MANAGING DEBT AND CREDIT

PUT DOWN THE SHOVEL AND GET OUT OF THE HOLE

"The rich rules over the poor, and the
borrower is the slave of the lender."

PROVERBS 22:7

CREDIT FREEZE

About fifteen years ago, my wife and I couldn't seem to get out of credit card debt. We realized if we wanted to stop digging the hole, we'd have to put down the shovel. We wanted to give up our credit cards, but we weren't 100 percent "in." So, rather than destroying them, we decided to freeze them. Literally.

We filled a Tupperware container with water and placed our two credit cards inside and put it in the freezer. It was a fun play on words—we were truly "freezing" our credit. We knew if we ever needed our credit cards, we could thaw them out, and there was an advantage to that process. We couldn't microwave the container or do anything to "unfreeze" the cards quickly, so we would have to think about our potential purchase during the thaw. It's fifteen years later, and we still keep our credit cards in the freezer as an important reminder.

When people are trying to get out of debt, they are less intimidated and more receptive to the idea of "freezing" their cards, rather than cutting them up. Freezing isn't as drastic a step, and they are more willing to end the cycle of debt.

STUDENT LOAN DEBT

According to the *Forbes* website *Make Lemonade*, there are more than 44 million borrowers with $1.3 trillion in student loan debt in the US alone. The average student in the class of 2016 owed $37,000.

That's sad to think about. There are young college graduates with close to $40,000 in debt. If they marry another college graduate, that young couple is potentially looking at $80,000 of student loan debt, not to mention they probably paid for a wedding, a new car, and a house. It's easy for young couples to rack up substantial debt before the age of twenty-five.

WAS IT WORTH IT?

I have a friend in her mid-forties who is still making student loan payments, and I also know a thirty-seven-year-old woman who is dealing with $100,000 of student loan debt. They are far along in their lives and careers, yet they are still carrying this burden. When I come across people in these circumstances, I find it interesting and I always ask, "Was it worth it?"

Sometimes, people reply that it was. Their degree helped them land their dream job, and they're doing exactly what they went to school for. Other times, people will say it wasn't worth it. They could have gotten their job without the college degree.

I think this prompts an important question for students who plan to attend college. "Am I studying to do what I really want to do?" I wonder if an eighteen-year-old is equipped to make that decision. They might think, "I have my whole life ahead of me. There's plenty of time for me to repay the loans. I'll make plenty of money once I graduate."

No parent I know wishes for their child to graduate from school with a large amount of debt, and no parent wants to see them repay loans for twenty or thirty years. If both parents and children plan and save in advance, it won't be that way. It enables the family to make sound decisions and possibly avoid student loan debt altogether.

THE START OF THE CYCLE

"Student loan" is a blanket term for any and all loans issued to pay for the cost of college.

Students don't just need money for tuition—they need money for books, food, clothing, housing, and living expenses. Many don't want to live a student's lifestyle if they don't have to, and when additional money is being offered, they figure they might as well take it. Reality hits hard after graduation, though, when former students realize they must begin paying off hundreds of thousands of dollars of debt.

Student loan payments are a long-term burden. We know students who took loans, didn't graduate, and ended up working part-time to pay off their debt. We also know people in their forties and fifties who are, absurdly, still carrying the weight of student loans. Some of these individuals end up taking on the debt of their children as well. When you're middle-aged, your focus should be saving for retirement, not paying off student loans from twenty years ago or taking care of your children's debts.

Taking out loans at an early age conditions young adults to acquire debt. It creates a mindset that borrowing money is acceptable and debt is okay. Since they already owe $50,000 in student loans, why not take out a car loan for $10,000? Debt becomes normal, and keeping track of the amount is no longer important. Since they're already in the hole, why should they bother keeping track of how deep it is?

It takes a long time to overcome such large, unnecessary

amounts of debt. It can have a tremendously negative impact on families—especially young families starting to have children. Not only that, but debt dictates certain decisions. The possibility of being a stay-at-home parent may not be an option because of debt. You may not be able to do certain things in life because you owe so much money. Debt can also make people commit to jobs or careers they don't enjoy, simply because they have to keep up with payments. There is a better way.

TIPS TO MINIMIZE STUDENT LOAN DEBT

Students can go to college without incurring a large amount of debt, and it starts with parents making and demonstrating sound financial decisions. With a little consideration and advance planning, you can minimize or eliminate the need for student loans.

COLLEGE ALTERNATIVE: A YEAR IN NORTH CAROLINA

I believe delaying going to college isn't a bad thing. Not everyone knows exactly what they want to do for a living when they graduate from high school. At the age of eighteen, many students don't have a plan, and that's okay.

My younger daughter and I had a conversation after she graduated from high school, and we agreed she wasn't ready for college. I wasn't willing to pay for her to attend school if she didn't know what she wanted to do. She said, "Well, I just won't go, then." I said, "Wrong answer." So, we came up with an alternative.

I grew up in North Carolina, and she always wondered what it would be like to live there. We decided she should move there and experience living independently for a while. It would also give her time to think about what she wanted to do in the future. Our plan was for her to find a job and a place to live, and she had to stay for at least one year.

The year she spent in North Carolina was a great learning experience for her. When she returned to California, she was ready to concentrate on college. Fast-forward two years, and she has an associate's degree. Living independently before beginning school is a viable option for young adults to avoid going into student loan debt, or at least keep the amount minimal. Parents can avoid spending money on a year or two of tuition for an undecided major. It can also be a period of additional savings for both the parent and the student.

START WITH THE END IN MIND: CHOOSE A MAJOR

Once a student decides to go to college, it's important for them to understand why they are there. Part of the reason I went to college was for the experience. There were vast social opportunities, and it was a time for me to practice independence, but I was also there to study and plan for my future. My parents did a wonderful job of helping me stay focused on that purpose. They explained that they had worked hard to save for my education, so I valued it and took it seriously.

When I started school, I was a general business major—I thought that would cover all my bases. However, I did well in my first accounting class, and my dad encouraged me to pursue an accounting major. He said, "Accounting is a great field. It will provide plenty of options for you after you graduate." I ignored his advice at first, but his voice of reason led me to change majors, and it turns out he was right.

Many of my peers changed majors multiple times. They chose majors based on the availability of classes, or what seemed interesting, not because they had clear direction. Some skipped and failed classes, and others were placed on academic probation, yet their parents kept paying for school. It was unfortunate to see students spend more and more of their parents' money by extending the time it would take to graduate.

TAKE ONLY WHAT YOU NEED: MINIMIZE STUDENT LOANS

We understand that for some, it is necessary to obtain loans in order to fund higher education. If you need to do so, you should do all you can to keep the amount minimal.

I once worked with a student getting ready to attend medical school. The price tag was about $40,000 per year or $160,000 over the course of four years. She applied for student aid and was approved for $80,000 per year to cover books, room and board, and other living expenses. So, she was looking at a higher price tag of $320,000 for school and the expenses she had not previously factored in.

This young student understood the numerical difference between these amounts, but she didn't understand the implications they could have on her life. She could potentially graduate from medical school with an additional $160,000 in debt, so we had a conversation with her family to discuss her options.

Her parents were aware of the situation and didn't want their daughter to leave medical school with this incredible burden of debt. They agreed to contribute money on a monthly basis to help with additional school expenses.

Working together, they were able to keep her loans down to the minimum $40,000 per year. They were proactive and helped their daughter graduate from school with a smaller amount of debt.

EXPLORE OPTIONS: ALTERNATIVE FUNDING

There are other options to explore when planning to fund a college education. Student loans are not the only way. I took Advanced Placement classes in high school, and by doing so, I was able to earn some college credits. Parents should also encourage high school seniors to apply for scholarships—many are available. My parents required me to apply for two per week the last quarter of high school. It was like an extra homework assignment! Thanks, Mom and Dad, just what every senior wants to be doing their last spring term.

I also worked throughout high school. Once senior year hit, I upped my savings and started setting money aside for future college expenses. My goal was to have enough saved, so I wouldn't need to work during my first year of college. I wanted the freedom to adjust to living on my own and focus on my coursework.

Another option to look into is attending community college. They offer general education courses that can be more affordable. I knew many people who either went to community college first or held dual enrollment at two schools. They took general education courses at a community college and did major coursework at the university.

A few of my college friends also participated in work-study. They worked part-time at the library, in the cafeteria, or around campus and applied the money earned toward their tuition.

EMPLOYEE ASSISTANCE PROGRAMS

Employee assistance programs are also a viable option, especially for students returning to college to finish bachelor's degrees, pursue graduate studies, or obtain other designations and certifications.

Typically, large companies are willing to help with the growth and development of their employees, and employee assistance may be a negotiable aspect of compensation during job interviews. Potential employers will be impressed by your desire to further your education and become a better employee.

BIG LENDING

It's very easy to obtain a student loan. Even if an individual's application reflects they have no income, no savings, and no employment history, banks will freely lend to that person. In fact, we've seen that it's easier for a college student to get a loan than it is for a hardworking or retired sixty-five-year-old with a solid credit history.

Getting into debt early preconditions you to accept it over your lifetime. A 2018 article on USAToday.com reported the results of a study. Up to 31 million Americans with credit card debt believe they will never pay it off and will die with debt.* Government and banks make funding education easy for everyone, but there's a steep downside to that convenience. Getting a student loan is a simple process, and the usual requirements for other types of loans don't apply.

> **DEBT HAS A LIMIT**
>
> Eventually, you *do* run out of debt capacity. Banks will stop lending to you, or you won't be able to get more credit. You will have to stop borrowing money at some point, or you will go through a bankruptcy proceeding.
>
> The problem is, the rope is very long. It can take a long time to reach that limit, and when you finally do, it can be very painful.

DEBT OVER THE LONG TERM

People often ask us, "Is it better to get a fifteen-year or a thirty-year loan?" We can use simple math and the example below to determine the answer.

---

*   Carrig, David. "31 million people believe they'll still owe credit card debt when they die." USAToday.com. January 13, 2018. https://www.usatoday.com/story/money/personalfinance/budget-and-spending/2018/01/13/paying-off-credit-card-debt/1023310001/.

INITIAL LOAN AMOUNT $250,000	15 YEAR LOAN	30 YEAR LOAN
Interest Rate	3.75%	4.125%
Principal & Interest Monthly Payment	$1,818.06	$1,211.62
Loan Term	180 Months	360 Months

Take the amount of a fifteen-year loan (in this case, $250,000), and multiply the monthly payment by 180.

$1,818.06 × 180 = $327,250.08

Then, multiply the amount of a thirty-year loan by 360, and subtract the fifteen-year loan amount.

$1,211.62 × 360 = $436,183.20

$436,183.20 – $327,250.08 = $108,933.12

The difference is the cost of interest, and usually, it's quite significant. This doesn't just apply to student loans. This is for all loans in general.

My dad explained this concept to my husband, and it changed his entire perspective on buying a home. My husband then decided to relay this insight to friends who had recently purchased a new home. He asked them the price of their home, and the duration of their loan. Then, he did the math and shared what they would actually pay over the life of the loan.

While my husband was inspired by his new revelations, I'm sure the new homeowners were less than impressed with his math skills. However, they did share that they hadn't thought about their loan in that way. We see the price tag on a home or the amount of a loan but don't do the math. We don't realize the full amount we end up paying over the lifetime of the loan.

CREDIT CARDS

Young adults don't just rack up student loan debt. Credit card debt is also incurred in college. It used to be easy for credit card companies to get students to sign up for cards. On move-in day, there were vendor tables with representatives lined up on campuses. "Sign up and get a gift card." Or, "Sign up today and get free rewards." It was easy for parents to sign up, give their child a card, and tell them they'd pay off the bill each month. Or students could sign up on their own, even though they weren't prepared for the responsibility.

Many of my peers carried credit cards in college, and they paid for pizzas, rounds of drinks—you name it. I can only imagine the expenses they accumulated through four years of spring break trips, pizzas, and new clothes. What felt like innocent fun at the time turned into stress once the bills came in the mail. Don't get me wrong: I liked going out for pizza, too, but since I had allocated "fun money" in my budget, I didn't pull out a credit card to pay for it.

Credit card companies position getting a credit card as a sign of adulthood. We give cards to young adults in a setting where they'll likely make the most immature decisions of their lives, and their parents aren't around to guide them. Using credit cards at that age creates debt that could negatively impact the next fifteen years of a young adult's life.

When the girls were young, I taught them the dangers of smoking, and I strongly discouraged such a habit. While my teaching methods may seem extreme to some, they were effective. Most parents I know wouldn't encourage smoking or frivolous debt. I believe using credit is equally as dangerous as smoking and equally as bad a habit. The world shouldn't view it as a sign of adulthood or success.

BUILDING CREDIT WITHOUT CARDS

One reason parents allow their kids to get credit cards is they believe their children need a credit history. While building credit history is important, a credit card isn't required to do so. There is a misconception that credit history must be elaborate, when the truth is, one or two bills or regular payments showing you are responsible, or a letter from a reputable source, are sufficient. There's no need to run out and get six different credit cards or create a strategy to increase your credit score. It doesn't need to be that complicated.

I didn't get my first credit card until after I got married at age twenty-three. Before then, I was able to build my credit history in other ways, like through my apartment rental history and paying utilities in my own name. A true reflection of good credit is not just the history. It's showing responsibility—having bills in your name and paying them on time.

SHOULD YOU USE A CREDIT OR DEBIT CARD?

Statistics show if you use cards for purchases, you will spend more money. If you go to the grocery store with one hundred dollars cash in your wallet, you certainly won't spend more than that—you can't. However, if you go in with a credit card, you don't have a limit in mind. Typically, we spend 18 to 20 percent more on groceries when we use a card.

WHEN IS DEBT OKAY?

There are certain times when debt is okay, but it needs to be reasonable. It should be proportionate when compared to your income and expenses. Debt is acceptable when buying a home, given that it will appreciate or at least hold its value; buying a home is an investment in your future. You can sell your house, get your money back, and pay off the debt. Mortgage debt is okay if it's within reason. We recommend fifteen-year loans, and we believe the monthly payment on a reasonable mortgage is no more than 25 percent of your after-tax, take-home pay.

We also believe it's okay to go into reasonable debt for certain major home repairs. But remember from our budgeting and savings chapters, you should anticipate these expenses and have a savings plan for home maintenance, repairs, and new appliances.

Reasonable debt also supports income opportunities. If you've explored your options and find that obtaining student loans is the only way to get yourself through school, then borrow the money. The debt may be worth it to further your education and allow you to pursue a solid career. Many people with established careers return to school to get a master's degree or to earn a secondary certification. If $20,000 in debt will increase your career opportunities tenfold, then the debt is justifiable.

WHAT ABOUT CARS?

Forty years ago, car loans had to be repaid within two to four years. Now, car loans can span seven, eight, or nine years. The payments are more spread out, so we think we can afford bigger and better cars, when in fact, we are just making additional interest payments.

It's important to live within your means and purchase cars you can afford. Nobody needs an $80,000 car to drive five miles to work every day. I knew a man who paid huge amounts of money on his car each month, so I recommended he sell the car. He asked me what he would do for transportation if he did.

I said, "You can buy a car for $2,000, if the only purpose of the vehicle is to get you to and from work." So, he sold the car, and instead of buying a new one, he borrowed one from a friend. Within four months, he had enough money to buy a car he could afford, and he was able to pay cash.

GETTING STARTED

You *can* get out of debt. You don't have to live with it, and it isn't as hard as you think to pay it off. As people begin to get out of debt, they often realize how burdensome it was for them. Paying others every time you receive your paycheck isn't a good feeling. It's liberating when you can get paid and know the money is yours.

PUT DOWN THE CREDIT CARD

The hardest part of getting out of debt is putting down the shovel. It's difficult to stop digging that hole. Many clients have told us they want to get out of debt, but they won't stop using their credit cards. The reasons they have for not quitting aren't justifiable. They don't want to give up points or airline miles.

The first step of getting out of debt is to stop using credit cards. Don't dig a deeper hole while you're trying to climb out.

A CLEAR PICTURE OF DEBT

The second step is getting a clear picture of your accrued debt. You must come face to face with it. Many of us have multiple credit cards, a couple of car loans, a mortgage, and maybe an outstanding student loan. As awful as the process might be, list all your debt on paper or in a spreadsheet. Adding it up to see how much you owe can feel overwhelming, but it brings clarity.

The Fair Credit Reporting Act (FCRA) requires each of the nationwide credit reporting companies—Equifax, Experian, and TransUnion—to provide you with a free copy of your credit report, at your request, once every twelve months.* Run a credit check on yourself to make sure you aren't forgetting anything. You might find a random outstanding bill from ten years ago. Checking your credit helps to make sure your picture of debt is accurate.

Running a credit check also helps you catch errors. When my wife and I first ran a check on ourselves, some canceled credit cards showed up as open lines of credit. It was unsettling to see cards we had canceled ten years prior show up on the report.

---

*   consumerftc.gov

RANK THE DEBT

Once you have checked all sources and have a clear picture of your debt, the third step is ranking it from the smallest to largest amounts. If you have six outstanding loans, list the smallest one first.

Tackle and pay off the smallest one first. As humans, we like to feel successful. Getting the smaller ones off our plate quickly helps build confidence in the process. It gives us a feeling of accomplishment, and it helps keep the momentum going.

From there, you'll create a debt schedule. Author and motivational speaker Dave Ramsey calls this the "debt snowball." The premise is that once you've paid off the first debt, the money that would have been applied to it is now applied to the second one—more money goes toward the second debt. Then, after the second one is paid off, those two payment amounts are applied to the third, and you continue to grow your monthly payments toward each debt.

These three steps are your action plan for climbing out of the hole. Face the debt, strategize, and chip away. You must have the mindset you will not go into debt any further. You must be committed. You have to make the choice to use cash and "freeze" those credit cards. Just like anything else in life, if you embrace this mindset and work hard, you will succeed. You can be free from debt.

STAYING OUT OF DEBT

It's easy to stay out of debt if you spend less money and live within your means.

ADJUST YOUR BUDGET

As we discussed earlier in the chapter about budgeting, a budget is not set in stone. There are certain occasions that may require you to spend more money. For example, when relocating, you might have to eat out more often or pay for more gas. By recognizing what season you're entering and adjusting your budget accordingly, it allows flexibility, so you don't resort to using credit cards.

Consistently using cash is another way to remain debt-free. If you only carry cash with you, you won't be tempted to use credit cards for purchases.

GIVE YOURSELF GRACE

Getting out of debt takes discipline, but you must also give yourself grace. We do the best we can when we are learning and starting something new. Your budget won't be perfect at first, and that's okay. It may take a few months of budgeting and revisiting goals before you hit your stride. It's okay to slip up—just don't quit. Get back on the horse. Give yourself grace so that you can commit to this process long-term.

BENEFITS OF PAYING OFF DEBT

Earlier, we shared the freedom that comes with budgeting. You will not find that freedom with debt. Taking out loans and charging items to your credit card puts you in handcuffs. You have much more freedom when you have money in the bank and can pay for what you want and need. There's a big difference in the way bank withdrawals and credit card payments play out over time.

Paying off debt helps you sleep better at night. There is tremendous value in knowing the money you earn can be used for your and your family's needs, rather than for a purchase you made ten years ago. Continuing to pay off a car loan after it's long gone is a mentally draining experience. When you are free from debt, it changes your attitude about life and work. You can make unbiased decisions about the future without being tied to payments.

None of us can just get out of debt and be done. It will take time. The measure of getting out of debt successfully is progress. Success breeds more success, so even a little progress is encouraging and beneficial. Don't give up your goal of becoming debt-free.

CHAPTER

5

BUYING AND RENTING

KNOW WHAT YOU'RE GETTING INTO

"Caveat emptor—let the buyer beware."

People think buying a home is a sign of success. We've "arrived," and we're living the American Dream as soon as we have a house, two kids, and a minivan. Or a young person experiences some success in their career, and buying a house is the next logical step. Young adults often feel pressured by family, friends, peers, and coworkers to become homeowners. This causes them to buy homes before they can afford them and before they are ready for the responsibility. We believe you should only buy a home if you want one and can afford it.

RESPONSIBILITIES OF HOME OWNERSHIP

There should be more education surrounding the responsibility of home ownership. It's important for people to understand the difference between buying and renting. Buying a home is a big financial step. Along with the mortgage, there are many costs that accompany home ownership.

For example, a young married couple just starting out in life decides to buy a $300,000 home. In addition to the mortgage, they will need to equip the home with $50,000 worth of furniture and appliances. Appliances aren't indestructible—most will wear out and require repair or replacement at some point. The couple will need an emergency fund and should be prepared to handle home repairs or appliance replacements at any time.

THE REAL ESTATE BIAS

Buyers often rely on a real estate agent to walk them through the process of selecting and buying a home. However, the normal process doesn't necessarily work in the best interest of the buyer. If you're a buyer, the agent doesn't typically work for you—they work for the seller. The agent is compensated based on a percentage of the sales price, so their duty is to serve the person selling the home.

There are excellent agents, but some are just interested in making a sale. Find an agent who will help you stick to your predetermined budget and price range and will research homes that fit within your parameters.

BORROWING TOO MUCH

It's easy to get approved for a home loan. Oftentimes, the amount a person gets approved for is much more than what they can afford. This can lead to problems, including foreclosure.

It can take years to overcome the devastating effects of losing your home when property values decline, pay is reduced, or jobs are lost. In the financial crisis of 2008–2009, I helped several families pack, load U-Haul trucks, and move into rental spaces due to financial trouble. This happened partly because they bought homes before they were ready, and when their incomes took a hit for various reasons, they couldn't sustain their loans. They were all wonderful people, and the events were unfortunate. They just weren't prepared for the downside of home ownership.

IS IT TIME TO BUY?

When making the decision of whether to buy or rent a home, consider your long-term and short-term goals. A home is a long-term investment, and it must be in line with short-term goals. For instance, if you know you are relocating in six months, you wouldn't want to buy a house—the time frame is too short, and it would be a risk to purchase a home.

When buying a home, you'll want to take a few qualitative

factors into consideration, such as whether or not you plan to live in the community long-term, the school district, the length of the commute to your job, and whether or not you plan to upgrade or renovate the house. These factors as well as others are important, but they are not always considered before buying a home.

FUTURE LIFESTYLE

If you're relocating or thinking about buying a home, take your future lifestyle into consideration. For example, you may not have kids right now, but if you plan to have kids in a couple years, is this the home you want to raise a family in? There is no need to rush into buying—take your time. Renting for a while in a potential neighborhood can be a safe first step before you make a final decision. It's important to do your research.

My husband and I visited close friends who had recently bought a house. They didn't research the area and moved in fairly quickly. Their home is cute, and they live downtown, so there is plenty to do for fun. But the house and area don't seem well-suited for children, and I know they plan to have kids in the future. The school district isn't that appealing, and the crime rate is high a couple of blocks away. Our friends may discover in the next few years they have outgrown their home, or they might want to live in a safer neighborhood for the sake of their kids.

FUTURE INCOME

Another factor young couples need to consider is how their income might change in the near future. If you don't have kids but plan to have them in the future, will one parent want to stay home? Could you still afford the house if you decided to transition to a single-income household?

Also, consider possible changes to your income over time. Most people make more money as they get settled into a career. Will the house provide the lifestyle you want over the long term? For example, if you like to entertain, is it well laid out for entertaining friends and family? Or do you anticipate other family members coming to live with you in the future?

> Due to personal experiences with elder care, my wife and I knew we only wanted a one-story when we bought our home. We've lived in our house for seventeen years now, and we can comfortably retire here.

CONSIDER ADDITIONAL COSTS

It's quite possible for you to afford a house but not be able to afford the upkeep. Some properties are so vast that you'll have to hire a gardener or a pool maintenance service. Monthly utilities for homes with high ceilings can be quite expensive. You need to be aware of these things before you buy a home. Pay attention to the age of the house and whether or not it might need significant repair in the years to come. These factors should carry some weight in your decision to buy a home.

TAX IMPLICATIONS AND CITY DEVELOPMENT

Sometimes it's appropriate to evaluate county and city taxes for certain properties. You should research tax structures for your particular area. There could be a significant difference in the expense of homes that are only two blocks away from each other.

It's also important to consider possible future development of an area before settling there. Our neighborhood looks nothing like it did when we first moved in seventeen years ago. There's been a tenfold increase in the population. There were certain streets where we could drive continuously because there were no stop signs or traffic lights, and now, there are multiple stops on the route. I advise researching future development plans for an area before buying a home.

COSTS OF OWNERSHIP

Home Owner
- Principal
- Interest
- Property Taxes
- Homeowner's Insurance
- Structural:
  - Maintenance
  - Repair
  - Improvements
- Homeowner Association Fees
- Pest Control
- Time Commitment
- Purchasing/Selling Costs
- Inspections
  - Realtor Fees
  - Closing Costs
    - Tax Gains/Losses
      - Neighborhood &
        Community Commitment

Rent or Buy
- Utilities
- Water
- Garbage/Sewer
- Cable, Phone, &
  Internet Services
- Appliances
- Maintenance:
  - Repair
  - Replacement
  - Furniture
- Landscaping &
  Yard Maintenance
- Cleaning

Renter
- Rent
- Renter's Insurance
- Minor Maintenance

We interviewed several mortgage lenders to get their take on the costs of home ownership. The following section is a combination of advice from those lenders and what we've learned from experience.

ADEQUATE DOWN PAYMENT

We believe it's appropriate to buy a home when you have enough money saved to put down a 20 percent down payment, which is enough to avoid private mortgage insurance. This insurance can add a few hundred dollars to your monthly mortgage, so an adequate down payment can save you money in the long run.

A home is typically viewed as an asset, which means it

has a future economic benefit. However, it could also be considered a huge liability with an economic downside. You will owe money on a home, and you could end up owing more than you intended to pay for it.

We know an individual who recently bought a $300,000 home and only put $3,000, or 1 percent, down. This person owes the bank $297,000 for the house. So in reality, the bank owns the home. With any slight change to the housing market, the house could become a huge liability.

PERCENTAGE OF NET INCOME

We recommend you don't secure a mortgage that exceeds 25 percent of your net income. (Twenty-eight percent is the typical benchmark a mortgage lender would give, but we advise a slightly lower percentage.) Also, this 25 percent is the recommendation for the *total* payment, including principal, interest, taxes, and insurance. Another term for this is *PITI*.

For example, if you make $100,000 each year and pay 25 percent in taxes, your after-tax, take-home pay would be $75,000. Your annual mortgage payment should not be greater than 25 percent of $75,000, or $18,750 per year.

FIXED VS. VARIABLE MORTGAGE RATES

We advise selecting a fixed, rather than a variable, mortgage rate. Nobody wants surprises when it comes to mortgage payments, and variable-rate loans can increase over time.

Let's say you purchase a variable-rate loan in a low-interest-rate environment. As interest rates rise, there is a possibility your mortgage payment could be substantially higher in subsequent years. If your original rate is 3 percent, and the following year 4 percent, that's already a 33 percent increase in your rate. In a high-interest-rate environment, if 8 percent increases to 9 percent, that's only a 12 percent increase. The change from 3 percent to 4 percent seems small, but this small change is a large percentage.

A fixed-rate mortgage gives you control. You know what the rate is now, and you'll know what it's going to be for the life of the loan. You can budget your family's income appropriately, and you don't have to worry about rate changes affecting your budget. A fixed-rate mortgage may cost a bit more, but that isn't always the case.

FIFTEEN-YEAR VS. THIRTY-YEAR MORTGAGES

We also recommend choosing a fifteen-year mortgage over a thirty-year one. Payments for a fifteen-year mortgage span 180 months, whereas the thirty-year payments extend over 360 months—that's a huge difference in the amount of money you end up paying for your home. For a detailed example, refer to the fifteen- and thirty-year loan comparison in Chapter Four.

Another reason to choose a fifteen-year mortgage is to avoid getting stuck with the payments for a long time. We've talked to people who want to pay off their mortgage by the time they retire—they were forty-five years old when they took out a thirty-year mortgage, and they had a goal of paying it off by the age of sixty. However, the mortgage will last until they are seventy-five.

PRACTICE THE PAYMENT

One mortgage lender we interviewed compared paying a mortgage to the concept of playing football. He said, "Fumble before you are required to pay it."

What he meant was we should "practice" making mortgage payments before we really have to make them. Set aside the monthly payment amount and pretend you are paying for a few months; you'll create a nice little savings fund, and you'll know whether or not you can truly afford the payment. Talking with a mortgage lender at your local bank for an estimate or using an online mortgage calculator will give you an idea of what your monthly payment will be.

A TEST RUN

I like the idea of practicing payments, especially for renters who are thinking about buying. It's a good test run to find out if you can truly afford a monthly mortgage.

THE MYTH OF HOME OWNERSHIP

Home ownership is a part of the American Dream, but the bank owns most of our homes when we take out large mortgages. The myth is that you own the home, but really, you don't for a long time, especially if you borrow too much money.

A BIGGER EMERGENCY FUND

In addition to the down payment and the mortgage, home-owners must establish a larger emergency fund. In the chapter about saving, we advise people to save three to six months of living expenses for the fund. However, when you own a home, you must add in the increased cost of home emergencies. You'll need to save more money than you did before.

Friends of ours purchased a home, and within a few months, the furnace broke. They had depleted their savings to make the down payment and pay for initial repairs, so they went several weeks in the middle of winter without heat until they could afford to replace the furnace. We advise having your down payment and full emergency fund ready before buying a home so that you can avoid situations like this one.

MISCONCEPTIONS OF RENTING

Some people think they are "throwing money away" by renting, and this simply isn't true. If you go on vacation, is it throwing money away to rent a hotel room for the night? No. You are a consumer. You're consuming a room because you need a place to stay. You're not putting money in a trash bag and tossing it in the dumpster. You are paying for shelter for the night. Are we throwing money away when we pay for internet, cable, or a cell phone? Do we throw money away when we buy a hamburger? No. Renting is paying for a place to live for the benefit of having a roof over your head.

People may also think they aren't building an economic benefit for their future by renting. They think they need to build equity in a home. However, buying a house before you are ready does not build equity. The individual in the previous example who put 1 percent down on a new home is not building equity. About 75 percent of every dollar paid for the first five to ten years will go to interest, not principal.

BENEFITS OF RENTING

There are many benefits to renting. The rental real estate market is much more transparent than the housing market, and it's easy to compare properties. It is market-based, so you know exactly what the competition has to offer. You don't have to engage in the minutiae of the housing market. If you want a two-bedroom apartment or a small house, it's fairly easy to rent one. Following are a few more benefits of renting.

- There are no property taxes, and repair and maintenance risks are low. You do pay a deposit, and you will lose it if you damage the property in any way, but if the dishwasher breaks, you won't need to replace it. That's the landlord's responsibility.
- There is flexibility in cost. If you lose your job, you can downsize quickly, or you can move to a different neighborhood if it's going to save you money.
- You have freedom to move. If a new job opportunity arises in another city or state, you are free to take it, since you aren't tied to a location. Renting can give you more options in career and life choices. If you own a home, you're tied to it.

OTHER BENEFITS OF RENTING

If you discover you're in a bad neighborhood or you have unpleasant neighbors, you can leave. The neighbors in the apartment below my husband and me were around-the-clock smokers. We couldn't open our windows without being overwhelmed by the smell of cigarette smoke. As this went on, we strongly considered moving. As renters, we had the option. Luckily, the smokers moved, and we were able to stay in our apartment.

Also, amenities are often overlooked as a benefit of renting. Our apartment complex has a gym; racquetball, tennis, and basketball courts; a pool; and a Jacuzzi. My husband and I couldn't afford a house with a pool, and we save money by not needing a gym membership. Amenities can be considered a money-saving benefit.

RENTING VS. OWNING A HOME

There are many benefits of renting, but there are risks as well. Here, we compare those risks to the benefits of owning a home.

- There's a built-in cost-of-living increase to rent, so the rate could go up each year. If you buy a home and have a fifteen-year mortgage, your payment is consistent and predictable. There isn't a cost-of-living adjustment with a mortgage.

- There's usually no pride of ownership in a rental property. You can paint, landscape, and take care of a home however you wish, but most renters we know will say, "Who cares? It's a rental. I'm only going to be here for two years. It's not my carpet, so I'm not worried about it."
- There's a possible lack of stability. After you purchase a home in the area you want, you can stay there. You don't have to worry about getting priced out of the market or wonder if the property will still be available to rent in the future.

We were renters when the children were young and in elementary school. We were forced to leave two of our homes. Both times, the owners changed their views on renting the space, and they gave us thirty days' notice each time. We had a lot of anxiety trying to find a new home in a short amount of time, and we dealt with unanticipated moving costs. We lost family stability by being forced to move, and both times, I wished we were homeowners.

If you have to move out because of reasons beyond your control, it could change the school your kids attend. This isn't a big deal when they're young, but for high school students, it might feel like the end of the world.

THINK ABOUT IT

We don't want to discourage anyone from home owner-ship. We want it to be the right financial decision for you and your family. Research the areas where you'd like to live, figure out the true costs, practice making mortgage payments, and evaluate whether or not buying a home is a sound long-term decision. Don't buy a home because of peer pressure or because an uncle says you should. Don't give in to FOMO.

Home ownership can be appropriate, and most people will eventually achieve it. But the consequences of buying a home you cannot afford and are not prepared for can become a financial nightmare. Keep the following things in mind when you're thinking about purchasing a home.

1. Your emergency fund should be three to six months of living expenses. Remember that your emergency fund may need to be a bit larger than before, due to the added costs of home ownership.
2. Put down a down payment of at least 20 percent.
3. Choose a fifteen-year fixed mortgage.
4. Your monthly mortgage payment should be no more than 25 percent of your after-tax, take-home pay. There are online calculators that can help you deter-mine how much you can really afford.

If you want to experience the American dream of home

ownership, put a lot of money down, get a short-term mortgage, and pay it off as quickly as you can. Do the work to make it yours. That's *true* home ownership!

CHAPTER

6

INSURING

PREPARE FOR THE UNEXPECTED

"An ounce of prevention is worth a pound of cure."

BEN FRANKLIN, FOUNDER OF THE FIRST MUTUAL
INSURANCE COMPANY IN AMERICA

The first interaction people generally have with finance is insurance. They obtain their driver's license and have an immediate need for auto insurance. Decisions about car or medical insurance are often made before starting savings plans. Insurance is not designed to be a windfall, and we don't buy it so that we can take unnecessary risks. Essentially, insurance is paying someone to take financial responsibility for the risk you and your family face, whether it's life, property, car, medical, or disability. Insurance is the friend that has your back, but there's an annual fee for that friendship.

UNDERSTAND YOUR POLICIES

You must understand exactly what type of insurance you

have and the terms of your specific policies. Many times, people buy insurance based on the price, not the coverage, so they might not know exactly what they are insuring for or against. Choosing insurance based on price will leave you over- or underinsured. Either you won't have enough insurance to cover the need, or you will pay more than is necessary for proper coverage.

NEVER ASSUME

We have seen homes destroyed in the midst of construction. Recently, rain caused major damage to a home in my neighborhood. The roof was being replaced, and the home was flooded during the rainstorm. The insurance company disputed the homeowner's claim, as they had not agreed to insure a home without a roof. Never make assumptions when it comes to insurance policies. Review each one thoroughly, and ask your agent questions if you don't understand something. Even if a change or event is temporary (such as roof replacement), it's best to make a phone call and ask about coverage.

When my younger daughter moved to Reno, I co-signed on a lease with her. I called my insurance agent and extended my homeowner's policy to also cover the rental agreement. All it took was a quick call to my agent. It didn't cost me anything, and I had peace of mind knowing I was fully covered if something happened at the apartment.

AN ONGOING RELATIONSHIP

You shouldn't meet with your insurance agent once and be done with them. I recommend at least one meeting per year to ensure that you are covered for life-changing events. There should be an ongoing relationship, and you need to remain connected. As your life changes and evolves, your insurance needs will, too.

THE PURPOSE OF INSURANCE

Before buying insurance, think of what it will cover and why you need it. We've seen several cases where couples are overinsured. Some have had as many as sixteen different life insurance policies, and many of them were duplicates or unnecessary.

DEDUCTIBLES AND PREMIUMS

Premiums are the cost of insurance. It's what you pay on a monthly, quarterly, or annual basis. Annual premiums are usually financed over a year.

Deductibles are the portion you pay if the insurance must be used. It can also be called coinsurance. It's your skin in the game—your participation in the coverage.

Deductibles prevent frivolous claims. If your deductible is higher, your premium will be lower; policies with higher deductibles will have fewer covered claims. The bigger your emergency fund, the more you can save on annual premiums. You will have emergency fund money available to meet the higher deductible.

ASPECTS OF INSURANCE

The scope of this book won't cover the ins and outs of all insurances, but we'll provide key points and aspects of the most essential types in the following section. Our goal is to address the *what, why,* and *when* of each insurance.

AUTOMOBILE INSURANCE

Auto insurance offers protection to two different parties—you as the driver or owner of the vehicle, and anyone you may get into an accident with. There are three main types of automobile insurance: liability, collision and comprehensive, and uninsured motorist.

- Liability insurance is state-mandated and will pay for expenses to the injured party in the event of an accident. It protects you if you hurt someone else or damage their property. It will not replace your car or pay for your medical expenses.
- Collision and comprehensive insurance pays for your damages or allows you to replace your car, if needed.
- Uninsured motorist protection covers you if your car is damaged or destroyed by a driver who does not have insurance.

HEALTH INSURANCE

Due to the high and increasing costs of medical care, it's vital to have health and medical insurance. Health insurance protects your quality of life. It provides a backstop against the very real and high cost of medical care if you or a family member becomes sick or injured. Health insurance also gives you access to doctors and medical treatment for preventive care and treatment at the earliest signs of illness. We don't think anyone should ever be without health insurance.

Health insurance coverage can vary by state and by policy

type. Most people obtain medical coverage through employer-sponsored plans—either through their workplace or their spouse's. Under current law, children and young adults can be covered under their parents' plan until age twenty-six.

If you find yourself between jobs, the Consolidated Omnibus Budget Reconciliation Act (COBRA) will allow you to continue your existing coverage, although it will be at your expense. COBRA can also be helpful to bridge the gap for early retirees who retire prior to the start of Medicare benefits.

HOMEOWNER'S AND RENTAL INSURANCE (PROPERTY INSURANCE)

Homeowners shouldn't be without homeowner's insurance. It's typically mandated by lenders. Most of the time, people opt for a policy that will replace a structure on their particular piece of property. If your home needs to be completely rebuilt, there's usually an amount allocated to cover living expenses during the period of time when your home is uninhabitable. Damaged or stolen possessions are covered as well.

If you're a renter, you will want rental insurance. Some properties even require it. It doesn't protect the structure of the building. Rather, it insures the products and personal possessions in your apartment or home. Clothing, equipment, and personal possessions are protected in the event of a fire or other damaging event. Rental insurance is fairly cheap, and it usually covers theft. We advise young adults to purchase homeowner's or rental insurance and make it a priority when moving into their own place.

A LESSON IN RENTAL INSURANCE

Four of my guy friends lived together in college, and while students were away for winter break, someone broke into their apartment. The place was ransacked. One friend had rental insurance; the others did not. The one with insurance was able to take inventory of what was missing, and he was reimbursed for those stolen possessions. The others had to accept the loss and replace items with their own money.

It's important for parents of college-aged students who are renting to make sure their kids have rental insurance. Have them get their own policy, or add them to your policy. This is another great learning opportunity for young adults. Introduce them to your insurance agent.

LIFE INSURANCE

There are many types of life insurance: whole life, variable life, universal life, term life, and more. We won't go into the details of each of these, but you'll want to discuss each type with your agent and determine which one is best for you and your family.

The primary purpose of life insurance is to replace lost income. It shouldn't be viewed as a windfall of money. It's especially important for a young family to have this insurance, because children are dependent upon their parents' income. Life insurance also provides benefits for a family who hasn't yet amassed savings for important family goals. It would be appropriate to use the insurance proceeds to pay off a mortgage, fund college, or allow a spouse to care for children in the event of a parent's untimely death.

You don't want to purchase life insurance when it isn't necessary. You also don't want to buy a policy on an individual whose death would not cause a significant loss of financial security. People have taken out life insurance policies on newborn babies, and it doesn't make sense. Parents don't depend on a baby to provide income.

Couples should have life insurance when they buy a home. If one spouse passes away in a two-income family, the policy can help pay the remaining mortgage balance. It's important that stay-at-home parents also have coverage. If they were to pass away, the surviving spouse might need to hire a nanny or others to help take care of the kids and home.

Lastly, purchase life insurance when you are healthy. If you enter into a situation where you desperately need it, you may have a hard time obtaining coverage. We recommend you buy it before it's too late.

HOW MUCH IS ENOUGH?

We are often asked how much life insurance a person should have. The answer varies based on goals, income, and accumulated assets. Take a moment to consider which of the following would be priorities if you or your spouse died prematurely:

1. Paying off the mortgage
2. Paying off other debt (such as car loans, student loans, and consumer debt)
3. Providing college funds
4. Paying living expenses for the surviving spouse and children for a period of time
5. Allowing the surviving spouse to stay home with the children

According to financial planning benchmarks, twelve to eighteen times gross earnings is the general guideline for how much life insurance coverage to purchase. However, as with any benchmark, a complete analysis should be done to determine what is appropriate for you.

THE IMPORTANCE OF LIFE INSURANCE

A family friend, Jason, was in his thirties when he discovered he had terminal brain cancer. He and his wife had a one-and-a-half-year-old and a newborn baby. Prior to his diagnosis, he decided not to buy insurance because he considered himself to be young and healthy. He didn't think he needed it. We worked with Jason, and during the next two annual benefit enrollments at his job, Jason was able to buy insurance through his employer. He didn't have to go through the medical screening process, since it was a group policy. We had to make sure he could work until right before his death; otherwise, he wouldn't get the life insurance.

Jason lived and worked for two more years. He was able to get the insurance benefit up to $200,000. Sadly, he passed away shortly after that. Had he purchased life insurance when he didn't think he needed it, he could have left his family in a better financial situation.

The other unfortunate aspect of this story is that Jason had to work until right before he died. He wasn't able to spend more time with family and friends, because he had to work to secure the life insurance he obtained through his employer. Having a life insurance policy gives peace of mind to you and loved ones. In the case of a terminal illness, valuable time can be spent together, rather than worrying about or working for the future.

DISABILITY INSURANCE

The purchasing rules of life insurance also apply to disability insurance. Buy it before you need it. The likelihood of becoming disabled due to an accident at home, work, or in an automobile is higher than the chance of dying prematurely, yet people tend to forget about this type of insurance.

Disability insurance is usually available through employer group policies, but the coverage might be a small amount. For those who are self-employed or feel their employer coverage is not adequate, an additional or supplemental policy can be purchased separately. It's important for young adults to have this insurance as soon as they are employed, earn an income, and begin providing for themselves.

Social security has a disability program, but it's very difficult to qualify for it. In fact, most applicants are automatically declined and must go through an appeal process. You shouldn't rely solely on Social Security disability coverage.

Disability can burden a family more than a death for a long period of time, and the financial impact can be terrible. If I were to become disabled right now, my wife would have to take care of me. She might not be able to work, and it would be very tiresome.

MAINTAINING YOUR LIFESTYLE

When Kelly's grandfather was in his fifties, he became ill with kidney disease. He had a high-paying job at the time. He had to go on dialysis, and he eventually received a transplant. He could no longer work. It's not unusual to see someone go on disability and never return to their job, or they only resume work in a limited capacity.

Kelly's grandfather lived for ten more years with no income from working, but he was able to stay in his house and live the same lifestyle for the remainder of his life, because he had saved and had a disability policy in place.

LONG-TERM CARE INSURANCE

With today's longer life expectancies, it's very likely you or your spouse will eventually need some type of care as you age. Long-term care insurance provides coverage for extended care in a nursing home or other long-term care facility if and when that time comes. When we first meet with clients, it is not uncommon to hear that one of their top goals is to maintain financial independence and not be a burden on their children. Long-term care insurance can help achieve this goal.

This insurance can be purchased on a per-day basis, meaning you can receive a specified amount per day, for a designated time period. You also have the option to purchase it for a lifetime, but we don't generally recommend that. We believe it's important to have this insurance, because long-term care expenses are high and variable, depending on your location.

A young professional is not going to be concerned with this type of insurance. People usually look into purchasing this when they are in their mid-fifties. However, young adults should have a conversation about it with their parents. Find out if they have this coverage, and what their plans are for the future.

Young people should also consider what would happen if they had to be responsible for an older parent who requires care. If caring for an aging parent is something they aren't willing or able to do, they might want to purchase this insurance.

PEACE OF MIND

We've worked with families who have purchased long-term care insurance for an elderly parent. Their logic is if their parent doesn't have money to pay for the insurance, they certainly won't be able to afford the cost of care when the time comes. Having this policy gives the adult child and aging parent peace of mind that they can pay for quality care if it's needed.

ESTATE PLANNING

Everyone needs an estate plan. Estate planning allows individuals and families to ensure their wishes are carried out in the event of their death. Proper planning minimizes taxes, allows for orderly transition of property to designated heirs or organizations, and arranges for care and support for dependent loved ones. There are varying levels of estate planning based on accumulated assets, personal wishes, and phase of life. A family law attorney can help you understand what documents you need, and he or she can guide you on proper legal protection as your family grows, as you age, and as you accumulate wealth.

I once sat at a table with ten family members of a client who had recently passed away. Every person believed they understood what the deceased wanted, and each person's understanding was different. My wife and I didn't want there to be any confusion upon our passing, so we created an estate plan. An estate plan communicates to your heirs what your wishes are regarding all you've accumulated in your lifetime, and how the funds and possessions should be disbursed. Estate plans should be clear and concise, and it's beneficial to discuss the details with family members in advance.

A few years ago, my wife and I presented black binders containing our estate plan to our daughters on Christmas morning. Kelly called it the "black binder of death."

Our parents wanted to make sure we understood their wishes, and that my sister and I were together for the discussion. They wanted us to hear the same information so there was no confusion. Mom and Dad let us know how they wanted to be cared for when they got older, and what their expectations were. My sister and I were able to ask questions if something was unclear. Although it was a weird Christmas gift, I'm thankful for the plan and the transparency of the details.

ENCOURAGEMENT THROUGH PLANNING

Part of the purpose of sharing our estate plan with the girls was to let them know they would not inherit money from me. I wanted them to live their lives and earn an income—not wait for me to die so that they could receive a lump sum of money. We wanted to encourage our children to pursue their dreams and make a life for themselves.

We tend to think estate planning is something only older adults need to be concerned about, but it's important for young adults and parents to do this also. If you have young children, you'll need to specify who will be their guardian in case something happens and you are unable to care for them. Go through the proper channels and get the right documentation.

You'll want to let the selected guardian know you have chosen them, along with your wishes and provisions for your child. What school would you like for them to attend? What will you leave behind financially to cover the expenses of raising your child? Get the details worked out in advance so that there are no surprises for the appointed guardian. Will the person you selected to care for the children also be responsible for financial management of the assets left to them? There are benefits and drawbacks to each option.

You might also want to consider the skills needed to care for the children, which are not the same as financial management skills. A good family law attorney can help guide you to the right answers for your family.

GETTING STARTED

While this chapter may feel dark and depressing, insurance considerations are an important step in proper financial planning. We recommend taking the following steps to determine your insurance needs.

1. Review your current insurance coverages. Gather information on policies you own and coverage you have through your employer.
2. Identify any areas that may be missing or lacking in coverage.
3. Set up a time to meet with your insurance agent and make it a habit to review policies annually.
4. Start thinking about estate planning. Remember, everyone needs an estate plan.
5. Talk to your parents about their plans. Do they have long-term care insurance? What type of care do they expect as they age? Do they have an up-to-date estate plan?

We don't want you to work hard to create the life of your dreams and see it fall apart, or have it threatened by an unforeseen event. Proper insurance coverage and estate planning can protect you and your loved ones from unpredictable events.

SHARING

ALIGN FAMILY EXPECTATIONS

"Family life is the backbone of mankind, and that life is dependent upon mutual giving, sharing, and receiving from each other. It entails the proper use of each other's successes and failures for mutual up-building."

MOTHER ANGELICA

When it comes to money, there is secrecy and a lack of communication among family members. In fact, many families are divided because of the issues surrounding money. Instead of uniting a family, wealth can pull them apart. Having open conversations early and often about finances can align expectations and goals among family members and help prevent arguments due to differences in priorities and perception.

OPEN COMMUNICATION

I have two daughters, and they are both wonderful and unique in their own ways. They have very different personalities, interests, and motivations. As a parent, I have their best interests in mind, and I always want to support them in their various pursuits. But because of their differences, our support is varied. This is something the girls haven't always understood or thought was fair.

I'm sure parents with multiple children can relate to this. My daughters said it was unfair when I helped one and not the other. I used these moments to remind them of all the ways I've supported them, and that parental support isn't always identical. I believe I treated them fairly, which doesn't mean I treated them equally. For example, just because I gave one child twenty-five dollars for gas, it doesn't mean the other is entitled to twenty-five dollars as well.

I've raised my girls to feel comfortable bringing up their questions and concerns about family finances. I'm thankful we are transparent about our financial situation and that we're supportive of our children. When conflict arises, we address it, try to reach an understanding, and move on.

ASK THE RIGHT QUESTIONS

Oftentimes, older parents don't want to tell their adult children about financial problems. When we ask clients if they think they will be responsible for the care of their parents, they say, "No, my parents are fine." But do they know that for a fact? Have they had a conversation with them? We know many adults who ended up caring for their parents unexpectedly, so it's important to be sure about finances.

Adult children may hesitate to have this conversation with the older generation, because they feel financial matters aren't any of their business. However, if they will be caring for their parents or helping them with money, they need to be informed and prepared before that time comes. It's unfortunate when the conversation never happens and the adult child resents their aging parents for the burden of their care.

ELIMINATE VAGUENESS IN ESTATE PLANNING AND INTENTIONS

We have heard it time and again about children and grand-children who are promised a special family heirloom, such as Dad's baseball card collection or some other asset of emotional or financial significance. Sometimes these promises are cherished inheritances that get passed down through the generations. Other times, and quite often, it's a statement made and quickly forgotten by the donor, but one not so quickly forgotten by the heir.

Miscommunications and vague statements like these happen quite often. Confusion and animosity between family members can escalate if an older parent or grandparent has separate conversations with multiple family members. Gifts and intentions should be made clear and put in writing.

When my husband and I were saving to buy a house, both sets of parents told us they'd like to help with the down payment. We appreciated this, but we began to wonder what that meant, exactly. Were they going to contribute $200, or $5,000?

We went back to our parents for clarification and verified their plans. Parents and grandparents should make their intentions clear regarding gifts and money from the start, but if there is any confusion, it's the recipient's responsibility to clarify. Once my husband and I had discussions with our parents, we were able to act accordingly and come up with an appropriate savings plan, factoring in their generosity.

DON'T BANK ON INHERITANCE

We know people in their sixties who have never saved and have said something like, "As soon as mom dies, I'll get a million dollars." This is a terrible mindset, and it leads to people living their lives in expectation of an inheritance. It's awful that some people are just waiting for a parent or grandparent to kick the bucket so that they can get their money.

People should live their own lives, and parents need to

set the expectation early on that their adult children can't rely on an inheritance. Or they should make it known they won't receive one. If there is wealth in the family, the assumption is that parents will leave money to their children. Even if that's the case, you never know what will happen in the meantime.

We had a client who was waiting for his mother to die, and she lived to be ninety-nine years old. She was homebound, had medical expenses, and required around-the-clock care for the remainder of her life. Her son was seventy when she finally passed away, and by that time, she had spent most of her money on medical care—there wasn't much left. Her son had been waiting his entire adult life for that inheritance, and now he's in a financial predicament.

LIFELONG TRANSPARENCY

What we see is not always reality. Sometimes a family living in an upscale neighborhood appears to be the perfect suburban family, but it's possible they're deep in debt, facing financial hardships, and steps away from losing their house, while the kids are completely unaware. Parents need to be honest with their children about the state of their family finances. Protecting or shielding children from the reality of budget limitations doesn't benefit them in the long run.

If parents allow their children to play three sports in a year and go on class trips to Europe, the kids will assume their family is wealthy. In reality, the parents might be racking up debt or neglecting to save. External circumstances can be misleading, so it's important for parents to inform children of their true financial situation.

ESTABLISH REALISTIC EXPECTATIONS

We know it's rare for an American family to have open and honest conversations about money. Parents usually don't want to share financial information with their children. There's an unspoken taboo against telling your kids how much money you make, and there's a problem with the "don't ask, don't tell" approach.

If you never discuss finances as a family, children could grow up with unrealistic expectations. They will have no idea what the family income is and no clue how much their parents pay for expenses. They will have nothing to compare their own income to and will try to maintain the lifestyle they had when they lived with their parents. If the parents drive a Mercedes, a new college graduate might expect to drive one as well. Many kids fail to recognize, however, that their parents drove a $400 Datsun when they were that age. It took them many years to accumulate enough wealth and financial security to buy a nice car, but the kids have no grasp of that concept.

Avoiding conversations about money also sets your children up for a shock. They won't be prepared for the cost of adulthood. They'll graduate from high school and be left in the lurch; financial concepts will be brand-new to them. If you have never disclosed information about your income and have paid for everything for your child's entire life, then your child will most likely have financial struggles when they are out on their own.

There are many ways for us to help our kids become financially responsible. A good place to start is by having honest conversations about money. Ask your kids how you can help them understand the value of money and become good money managers.

FAMILY PARTICIPATION

For young families with small children, conversations about the budget, limitations, and expectations should be a regular occurrence. For instance, a conversation about what you can spend on dining out each week is a good start. As a parent, you can say, "We have enough money to go out to eat twice this week." You don't have to give specifics and tell your kids exactly how much money is budgeted for the week—just share general information.

Having open conversations creates a healthy ideal in young children's minds about money and budgeting, and it teaches them the value of planning ahead. Instead of arguing with a child who wants to go to McDonald's every day, you can simply say, "Remember, we talked about this? We planned our budget, and we're only going out to eat twice this week."

As children get older and begin to need money to go out with friends and for extracurricular activities, the discussions become more concrete. They are directly involved in the conversation, and costs can be shared. "The cost for cheerleading this year is $1,000. We may need to make some changes in our budget to pay for this, or we'll need you to contribute a certain amount from your part-time job."

When children become adults, sharing is less specific. Honest sharing is important, but it's perfectly acceptable to maintain a level of privacy. A seventy-year-old parent doesn't need to show their tax return to a fifty-year-old adult child.

Older parents don't need to share how much money they make, but adult children should know if their aging parents are in need of financial support. If you are an adult child with older parents and this hasn't been discussed, we suggest you have this conversation so that there are no surprises in the future.

Having financial discussions early and often sets a realistic expectation of what your family can afford, and it makes children part of the process. If this isn't something you have been doing, you can start now. Planning, budgeting, and saving model good behavior, and when children are involved in the process, they are likely to adopt the same behavior. These conversations aren't rigid or intimidating. They bring families closer together and establish a healthy pattern for life.

PARENTING NEVER ENDS

The relationship between parents and children changes over time. Parents do less instructing and more offering of counsel and advice. When an adult child is making a decision or entering a new phase of life, the parent might say, "Would you like my opinion?" or, "Can I share my experience with you?" This is a much better approach than offering advice that may not be wanted, and it's more likely to be well received.

In another fifteen years or so, my role and Kelly's role will be reversed. The roles have already reversed in the relationship with my mother. I don't tend to ask my children for advice, but my mother comes to me for it. I know there will come a time when I go to my children with questions. I hope we are able to continue having conversations from a position of mutual respect—we have differing knowledge and experiences, and both sets are valuable. Open communication creates a lifetime of conversations that go back and forth, and it's not just about the role of parent and child. It facilitates the gradual changing of the roles and helps us easily recognize who leads and who follows in each one.

SUPPORTING ADULT CHILDREN: WHEN IS IT TOO MUCH?

We know an adult child in his mid-thirties who has been telling his parents that his big break is just around the corner. He's passionate about what he does, but unfortunately, he's pursuing a job in a very competitive industry. His parents send him thousands of dollars each month to cover his rent and living expenses. Like many young adults, he has expectations surrounding the career he thinks he should have, and he's not working in the meantime to provide for himself.

It's risky for these parents to continue sending money to their son. They are retired and in their seventies, and they aren't earning an income to replace the money they send him for support. This story might seem like it's unique, but parental financial support of adult children is a regular occurrence.

More and more, we see older parents delaying their retirement because of choices their adult children have made. Kids are "forcing" their parents to continue working, and it's draining their money when they need it most. The parents of adult children might be taking care of elderly parents or grandparents, saving for retirement, or paying for their own advanced medical care. They simply can't afford to support their adult children, too.

I hosted a lunch for a group of financially independent, retired women. This lunch provided a forum for brainstorming sessions and for the ladies to share pressing financial concerns and challenges.

These women are some of the most financially literate and savvy people I have ever met. However, through our discussions, I found out nearly all of them were paying all or part of the living expenses for a child or grandchild. They didn't like doing it, but they didn't know how to stop, either. Some of these women were in their seventies and paying expenses for adult children in their fifties. One middle-aged child was out of work, and another had recently divorced. These women didn't want their adult children to be financially destitute or kicked out of their homes, but they didn't know how to stop the payments without creating disharmony in their families.

Parents and grandparents tell me they feel obligated to help their children financially. They have the money, so they feel guilty if they don't contribute. Losing a job and getting a divorce are both unfortunate events, but the older generation *should not* have to take care of the younger one financially.

I believe part of being an adult is taking care of yourself—that should be your number one goal. Pursuing passions and other interests is secondary to making sure you have a place to live and food on your table. You may need to work extra hours, study late at night, or spend time on the weekends building your skills for that dream career.

I can't remember the last time I had to ask my parents for money. I take pride in how hard my husband and I work to provide for ourselves. I know my parents would lend a helping hand if we were in dire need, but I would come up with other ways to make ends meet before asking my parents for monthly support. It's no longer their responsibility to make sure my daily, basic needs are met.

TEACH THROUGH EXPERIENCE

None of us begins our financial journey perfectly, and sharing negative experiences or unwise decisions from the past can help steer your child away from making the same mistakes. When we first meet with a client, we ask, "What was the worst financial decision you've ever made?" They usually laugh at themselves, and then share it. Then, we ask, "What was the best decision?" This one is more difficult for them to answer; they have to put some thought into it.

Bad decisions are painful, so they stand out in our memory, whereas the ways we may have diligently saved do not. Saving is a big success, and that should be shared—parents need to recall good decisions and positive experiences, not just the bad ones. Sharing successes can inspire and encourage your children to model those behaviors.

CONSTANT COMPARISONS

People often ask us how they are doing compared to other people their age or to others in the same profession. Even a couple in their fifties with a net worth in the millions will ask, "Are we doing okay compared to others? Do we have enough?"

This questioning doesn't begin suddenly once a young adult gets a job, or when an older adult prepares for retirement. We believe part of the reason for comparisons are the expectations people had about money as children, and the lifestyle they are accustomed to while living with their parents.

It's hard to have a sense of how we are doing when we wrongly compare the successes of our mid-twenties to those of our parents—it's comparing apples to oranges. It took our parents years to climb the career ladder, buy their dream homes, and vacation first-class. We can't put so much pressure on ourselves, and we certainly can't expect to live like an established middle-aged adult at the age of twenty-five. Ask your parents where they lived and what their lives were like at your age. It might help you gain perspective.

Think of the average American family thirty-five years ago. It was common to have one car back then. Today, many young families have two cars, so they have twice as many vehicles as their parents had. Many young adults grew up in apartments or rental properties that may have been 1,000 square feet, but their own children have lived in a house since the day they were born.

I grew up with a solid understanding of what it costs to live in the world. I didn't know the dollar amounts of my dad's paychecks, but I knew if we could afford to go out to eat that week or play multiple sports that year. As I got older and we had more candid conversations, I wasn't shocked to find out how much it costs to live independently as an adult.

IDEAS FOR THE FAMILY

There are many ways to get your whole family involved in the family finances, and we've outlined a few ideas below. The family conversations don't have to start with a formal review of the budget—they can be as simple as involving the kids in planning the annual summer camping trip. Start having fun conversations with your family about money and finances, and let your kids see that money doesn't have to be a stressful or taboo conversation.

CHARITABLE GIVING

Beyond having conversations about finances, families can set goals together. The one thing we like to do as a family is give money to charity; it doesn't matter if it's only a small amount. We talk about what's important to us, and we give to organizations that align with our family values. The practice of giving establishes it as a priority.

Giving does not have to be monetary—it can be time and service as well. Our family has given to charity, but we've also worked at charitable events. We've served at food banks, collected items for local homeless shelters, and even built homes together. It was all time well spent as a family, while helping our community. Giving, volunteering, or doing service projects is beneficial on more than one level, and it brings a family closer together.

PLAN A FAMILY VACATION

Planning a vacation is another way to encourage family participation in financial decisions. It's fun to decide where you're going, and everyone has a say in how to enjoy the money.

For example, once you've determined the destination, let each person decide on an event or attraction they'd like to visit, and find out how much it will cost. This allows everyone to see what's available in the vacation budget, sets expectations, and helps create an itinerary. If a particular event will stretch the budget, everyone is aware and can plan what is affordable. Also, there won't be a credit card bill waiting later on.

You can also plan a vacation well in advance and save for it. Figure out how much the trip will cost and how much it will cost to visit each attraction. The entire family can budget and save for the trip, and it will be rewarding for everyone.

CHORES

Parents care for their children, but younger kids should still have responsibilities in the home while they live there. Cleaning their room, doing dishes, and taking out the garbage are examples of some basic chores they can do. And it makes sense that their responsibilities should increase as they get older.

We believe that doing basic chores to maintain the home should be an expectation of children living in the house; there's no payment for those. However, they can be given opportunities to earn money through additional chores— we call that commission, rather than allowance.

I don't want to sound harsh, but I don't think children should get paid just because they live in their parents' house. Children receive the benefits of a roof over their heads, warm food, clean clothes, and a comfortable bed. Those things aren't free, and basic chores should be done to share in family responsibility. I believe if a child wants something outside of what is normally provided, they should earn it. I'm a big proponent of children understanding the value of working for money.

While growing up, my sister and I had basic chores that were mandatory, and optional chores we could do to earn money. My sister used to pay me to do her chores, and I was fine with it. If I cleaned her room, she gave me her money, and Dad didn't see anything wrong with that. After all, we pay people to mow the yard and provide other services for us. We learned the value of working to earn money, and we both learned how to negotiate business deals.

START THE CONVERSATION

Being open about finances eliminates confusion. If you have the opportunity to start early, you should. Demonstrate to your kids that money is part of everyday life. And remember, the responsibility doesn't fall on the parents alone—adult children need to ask questions when appropriate. We hope the suggestions shared in this chapter have encouraged you to begin having conversations about finances with your family.

CONCLUSION

"Don't become a wandering generality. Be a meaningful specific."

ZIG ZIGLAR

We've covered a lot of information in this book, but it doesn't have to be overwhelming. We haven't created a new system, and everything we suggest has been done before.

We make financial decisions multiple times each day, and we'll continue to do so for the rest of our lives. Whether fresh out of college or entering retirement, we need a framework to make those decisions wisely. We need tools, ground rules, and support from family and friends. We've laid out the ground rules in this book. You can do these things and live a better life. Establish your targets, and you don't have to wander.

We've provided many ideas, tools, options, and resources for improving your financial life, but we don't suggest implementing them all at once. Choose an area you're unhappy with, or one that doesn't align with your vision and goals, and start there. Once you tackle that one, you can begin to make another change. If the thought of budgeting paralyzes you, then start with saving—don't try to do everything right away. Just get started.

ENVISION THE FUTURE

I believe the reason my husband and I have been financially successful is we spend a great deal of time envisioning our future and talking about it. Right now, we're planning to welcome our first child into the world. We discuss traditions we'd like to begin, like what we want to do each Christmas; we want to take certain vacations and give our kids a variety of experiences.

Find your "why"—your purpose. Cast that vision for yourself and your family, then align your finances to the vision. Once you have a vision and clear goals, decisions are easier to make. You can ask yourself, "Does this choice line up with what I've envisioned for my family?" If not, you won't waste another minute thinking about it. If it does, you will move forward with an action plan. You'll determine if you need to save or begin doing something differently.

FINDING AN ADVISOR

If you're looking for a professional financial advisor, look for someone who has aboveboard credentials, like a Certified Financial Planner®. You can find financial advisors online, and you can check national databases like FIN-

RA's BrokerCheck to confirm credentials and view their history. You can see if there have been any complaints against the advisor.

When you meet with an advisor, find someone who wants to teach and guide you, not one who is just trying to sell you something. There are many people in this business who truly want to help their clients lead better financial lives.

CHECK THEIR VALUES

You'll also want to find an advisor who is supportive of your vision and goals. Don't meet with a professional who serves the opposite of your vision.

For example, we don't work with gamblers or moguls—people who want to get rich trading, or who just want to accumulate money and power. We work with family stewards—people who want to make good financial decisions to benefit their family. We focus on family needs and find solutions based on those needs, rather than giving a set of rules to a client about what they can and can't do with their money.

THE NEXT THIRTY DAYS

When I teach classes, I ask, "How many people in this room

think they could implement a decision that will destroy their life over the next thirty days?" Many believe they could. They could spend too much money or go into debt. So why couldn't we also make decisions that would make our lives *better* over the next thirty days?

If you've made poor financial decisions in the past, leave those behind and start over. You can start with a fresh slate and cast a new vision. You're never doomed to stay in a bad financial situation. Envision a better life for yourself and start making those decisions. You'll be better off in thirty days, even better off in ninety, and exceptionally better off in two years. Commit to changing your habits and begin the process of change.

FINAL WORDS OF ENCOURAGEMENT

If your family is one that views talking about money as taboo, we're here to encourage you to begin having conversations about finances. Open, honest communication will bring a family closer together, even if it's uncomfortable at first. The more you talk about it, the more natural it will become.

Our advice to young adults is not to be discouraged. It takes time to build wealth, and if you are in your twenties, you are just getting started. There's more opportunity today than ever—there's so much more you can do, and you have time to build that savings account, start a college fund for your kids, and invest to grow your money. So, what are you waiting for? It's time to get started!

ABOUT THE AUTHORS

TERRY LINEBERGER learned the value of saving while growing up in a poor, single-parent household in North Carolina. As a CPA and Certified Financial Planner®, Terry strives to stay up-to-date with the ever-evolving world of finance. He is a well-respected advisor specializing in helping manage the wealth of multi-generational families.

KELLY LAUTERJUNG is a financial advisor who inherited her passion for financial planning from her father, Terry. She graduated from the University of Oregon with a bachelor of science in accounting and then worked in corporate America before partnering with her father.

Made in the USA
Lexington, KY
11 November 2019

56761387R00107